MAIN LIBRARY
ALBANY PUBLIC LIBRARY

MAIN LIBRARY
ALBANY PUBLIC LIBRARY

NAPOLEONIC PLASTIC FIGURE MODELLING

NAPOLEONIC PLASTIC FIGURE MODELLING

Bill Ottinger's HISTOREX MASTERCLASS

Windrow & Greene

© William F. Ottinger 1997

This edition published in
Great Britain 1997 by
Windrow & Greene Ltd
5 Gerrard Street
London W1V 7LJ

Colour Separations by In-House Colour

Printed in Spain by Graficas Reunidas SA

Designed by Tony Stocks/TS Graphics

All rights reserved; no part of this publication may be reproduced or transmitted in any form or by any means electronic or mechanical including photocopy, recording, or in any information storage and retrieval system, without the prior written consent of the publisher.

A CIP catalogue record of this book
is available from the British Library

ISBN 1 85915 019 5

CONTENTS

Preface & Acknowledgements..6

Introduction: The Historex Story
Eugéne Lelièpvre & Lynn Sangster...............................9

Chapter One: The Figure Line...................................18

Chapter Two: Assembly, Detailing & Enhancement.....29

Chapter Three: Converting..56

Chapter Four: Painting..78

Chapter Five: Groundwork & Display........................107

Chapter Six: Non-Napoleonic Conversions.................117

Note on suppliers..127

PREFACE & ACKNOWLEDGEMENTS

The Napoleonic era remains one of the most popular historical periods for military miniaturists and collectors. Its popularity is due to any number of factors: the dazzing array of uniforms, the larger-than-life personalities, the dramatic military history of the period, and its sheer élan - the years between 1793 and 1815 saw countless adventures by land and sea which in sober retrospect seem almost too astonishing to believe. The uniforms reflected the era's flamboyance, which arguably produced the epitome of military splendour. Extraordinary sartorial displays - dark blue cuirassier coats with pink facings; yellow hussar pelisses richly trimmed with fur; green dragoon coatees faced with all the colours of the rainbow, and worn with gleaming brass helmets; nodding plumes, tasselled boots of supple red leather, gold lace and braid by the yard - graced battlefields from Portugal to Moscow, and from the North Sea to Egypt.

The absence of photography left us only paintings, sketches, written descriptions and a few precious surviving uniforms from which to recreate this visual perspective; but today it is possible to create detailed three-dimensional miniatures which surpass in immediate appeal most impersonal museum displays. The Historex line offers the miniaturist an unusual opportunity to recreate any military aspect of the period (as well as a limited array of civilian subjects). The company's dedication to precision and diversity has produced an enormous number of figures and parts. In the hands of the modeller hungry to create something individually appealing, Historex is both a challenge and a delight.

Incorporated into historically accurate vignettes and dioramas, these individual figures or scenes often evoke from the casual spectator a response of amazement. This reaction is largely due to the fact that everything "just looks right"; and the main reason is the sheer number of parts which make up a single Historex figure - the model of a mounted cavalryman may be assembled from well over a hundred parts. Even given the enormous advances in metal and resin castings, no other medium can equal the detail.

Whether military miniatures represent true "art" is not the issue; they are not meant to vie with the work of artists such as Meissonier, Detaille or Vernet, but rather to represent the colour and drama of military history in a three-dimensional form. For the painter and modeller desiring to create Napoleonic figures Historex offers a high degree of accuracy and superbly specific detail; for instance, the company provides scale mouldings of *two different* degrees of the French Legion of Honour decoration, each measuring less than three millimeters in length! The firm continues to manufacture a far-ranging line of kits, expanded in recent years to include a growing number of special parts for conversion work and dioramas.

APPROACH & CONTENTS

The information and illustrations in this book are presented at two levels. For the Historex novice there is a basic primer on assembling these somewhat complex figures. For the more experienced or adventuresome modeller, there is a detailed section on conversions. Augmenting these chapters is another on painting Historex; while there has been a recent spate of books and articles on painting miniatures, Historex presents special challenges and rewards, and is a step beyond the buy-it-and-paint-it realm of figures. This is followed by a chapter on groundwork and display methods to set off the finished miniature to best advantage. While this book deals almost exclusively with the Napoleonic era, there have been countless examples of impressive Historex conversions to subjects outside that period, and no study of Historex can properly omit this aspect. Without pretending to do this area justice, the last chapter provides the reader with an idea of what can be accomplished through illustrations which amply convey the conversion possibilities open to the more adventurous.

The author has spent the past twelve years working almost exclusively with Historex, specializing in Napoleonic cavalry and conversions. Several books have recently been published on the building and painting of miniatures; two which especially come to mind are Shep Paine's *How To Build and Paint Scale Figures* (Kalmbach), and *Bill Horan's Military Modelling Masterclass* (Windrow & Greene). Both contain sections applicable to Historex; and instead of rehashing the more basic material already covered in these excellent publica-

PREFACE & ACKNOWLEDGEMENTS

tions, the information presented here is intended to supplement them, adding information that is Historex-specific. More to the point, most of the emphasis in this book is upon mounted figures.

Included throughout the text are observations by some of the best Historex modellers and painters in the world. Painting styles may vary dramatically, but all have produced superb figures. Throughout these sidebars there is a repeated theme of admiration for the detail and accuracy of Historex products; of recognition of the inherent conversion possibilities; and, particularly, of admiration for the horses, representing Historex's pioneering contribution to up-grading the hobby beyond static figures. Each painter has briefly noted his personal experiences in working with the figures. What becomes obvious as you read these observations is an unbridled enjoyment of what was initially a revolutionary modelling medium; and even - if you read carefully between the lines - what can only be called a fondness for these particular pieces of plastic. This is unique in the world of military miniatures.

Our overall hope is that painters, collectors and enthusiasts of the Napoleonic era will enjoy the collection of photographs, which will provide the strongest attraction for many readers. They illustrate work by some of the world's top military miniaturists, spanning a period of more than 30 years and covering a wide range of subjects. Both stock and heavily modified figures have been selected, as well as some radical conversions to totally new subjects. Wherever possible the subject, painter and photographer have been identified; regrettably, however, the span of years has left a few photographs unidentified. It is hoped that the appeal of the subject matter and quality of the work will atone for these few lapses in identification.

ACKNOWLEDGEMENTS

There is never a truly effective way to thank the many individuals who assist in the preparation of a book. So many people contributed, both at inception and during all the years leading up to the decision to bring it all together. There were many who suggested that I write a "Historex book", and others who provided encouragement, suggestions and material as thoughts were put onto paper. The very close fraternity which exists among figure painters became obvious from the gratifying responses I received whenever I voiced particular needs. Like so many others who create a book, I feel a certain degree of guilt in taking credit as the "author".

My sincere thanks to two special friends must be recorded: Mike Hall and Roger Becker laboured through the early drafts and performed yeoman duty as editors, transforming an erratic stream of consciousness into order and clarity. Special gratitude also goes to Shep Paine and Bill Horan, both for their pioneering work and for their own books, which have advanced the hobby. In these days of the large scale metal and resin figure, they have proved time and again the astonishing things that can be accomplished with small scale plastic figures. I owe a long-standing debt to Shep for his patience, translating abilities, practical suggestions, and constructively critical eye over the years.

I also want to thank a group of talented painters whose work was the early spark for my own interest in Historex. These include Peter Twist, Andrei Koribanics, Larry Munné, Joe Berton and, of course, the godfather of America's discovery of Historex - Shep Paine. On the other side of the Atlantic, the Historex creations of Max Longhurst, Dr Mike Thomas, Graham Bickerton, Ray Lamb and Bill Hearne served to whet my budding interest. I particularly want to thank Lynn Sangster of Historex Agents, Dover, Kent, for his help and suggestions in preparing this book. Lynn's Historex distributorship continues to be a linchpin for these figures. Dominique Breffort of Histoire & Collections, Paris - the publishers of *Figurines*

PREFACE & ACKNOWLEDGEMENTS

magazine - was instrumental in locating many of the photos, passing the word to European painters that a book on Historex was in the making, and encouraging them to contribute. Christian Sauvé, owner of NCO Historex, should also be saluted both for his company's continuation of the line and for his generosity towards me.

A very special thank you must go to the greatly respected Eugéne Lelièpvre for his help and correspondence during the preparation of this book. He is truly the father of Historex, and its many admirers owe him more than can be repaid. His knowledge of Napoleonic uniforms, equipment and equine subjects were perfectly blended with his demands for accuracy from the earliest days.

The collection of photographs is the result of the generosity of many painters and collectors who patiently endured my nagging for photographs from their collections and my requests for help in identifying the work of other painters. At the risk of leaving someone out, my thanks on this score to: Chris Casazza, Phil Cranz, Greg DiFranco, Dr Chris Durham, Bill Horan, Nick Infield, Phil Kessling, Martin Livingstone, Max Longhurst, Shep Paine, Ivo Preda, Dr Preston Russell, Lynn Sangster, Claudio Signanini, Philip Stearns, Lane Stewart, David Stokes, Ron Souza and Dr Mike Thomas. My thanks also to Dick Pielin for the loan of irreplaceable Mokarex figures from his collection.

Finally, special thanks to my wife Sandra for her non-modelling editing, which resulted in practical modifications to the text. Her support goes beyond what most "figure widows" endure through their husbands' dedication to the hobby. In the process she has come to appreciate Historex and to be even more patient with my own fascination for these marvellous figures.

Bill Ottinger
St Louis, MO
December 1996

INTRODUCTION:
THE HISTOREX STORY

There are two names which are today almost synonymous with Historex. In distinct and different manners, both Eugéne Lelièpvre and Lynn Sangster have been instrumental in the history of these figures. Maitre Lelièpvre - born in 1908, a pupil of Benigni, a brilliant model-maker, a respected equine artist, and an official Painter to the French Army for more than 45 years now - was the designer and guiding light for the original moulds, adding his vast wealth of uniform knowledge to their development. His input resulted in a degree of accuracy that few manufacturers or designers can match today. Lynn Sangster, after becoming fascinated with Historex, was chosen as the primary distributor. His colour catalogues not only successfully promoted the line but have become collectors' items in their own right. For those reasons and many others, no publication focusing on Historex can be complete without a word from each of these men who have made such contributions to the military history hobby.

The Creation of Historex Figures: Eugéne Lelièpvre

I have always been interested in horses and soldiers. Even as a child I preferred to draw and cut out my own paper soldiers rather than use the printed Epinal ones. All those horses walking exactly the same way seemed so unrealistic to me.

In 1935, like everyone else, I was painting flat figures. I was a member of the Societé des Collectionneurs de Figurines Historiques, but at that time flats dominated the hobby and round figures were limited to the charming but naive figures produced by Mignot and Britains, which even the best painting could not transform into true historical figures. Several of us (I think I am the only one still living) wanted to make round figures that would be different from the toys - models which would be as good as the flats. We made plaster moulds and, as a specialist in animals, I was chosen to make the horses. After several attempts I produced a horse that was well received, even if it turned out to be a bit larger than intended. This is where the Historex 56mm size originated.

By 1960 I had a certain amount of experience with round figures. For 15 years I had been doing commission work for a rather demanding collector, amounting to some 600 pieces. This collector soon became one of my best friends - his collection was also mine! Financial difficulties forced the friend to look for ways to raise money, and he decided to take a part of his collection and reproduce it, selecting Napoleon's staff as his first project. The work was sent off to toolmakers, but my friend soon realized that the project was not financially feasible and abandoned it, forfeiting the work already completed (a nearly finished horse) to the toolmakers.

I think I can honestly say that I was the creator of Historex, for without me Historex would never have existed. I persuaded the managers of the toolmaking firm to embark on a new venture, the almost finished horse serving as a test. I agreed to provide the patterns and documentation if the test was successful; so Historex was begun in my studio. Napoleon's staff required too many figures for a test run, so we decided to start with a single subject, a hussar. Even though it was far from perfect it was well received, and we decided to go ahead with others.

My patterns were all made in lead and detailed as finely as possible to reduce the work required of the engravers, thus both reducing the cost and preserving the character of what I was trying to achieve. The engravers had only to add the details such as buttons and braid, as well as the final polishing of the moulds and cutting of sprues for the plastic. I provided detailed drawings for the engravers and supervised the work from start to finish. It was rare

INTRODUCTION: THE HISTOREX STORY

(Above) The forerunners of Historex kits were this line of Mokarex figures - here, Napoleon and Gen.Kellerman - originally packed as promotional gifts in coffee containers. (Courtesy Dick Pielin)

for me to be completely satisfied, and I soon acquired the nickname among the engravers of "Monsieur Yes, But. . ." - the engraving was long, hard work, and I was always demanding more, looking for ways to make the figures more accurate.

At the same time I developed the drawings and text that accompanied the kits. Writing the text, for example, required numerous drafts to distill all the required information down to fit, whenever possible, onto a single sheet. The drawings for the colour cards included in the kits were also complicated, requiring several sketches to ensure that all the necessary details could be seen. Today, I am still proud of the assembly of serious reference material they represent. Over a 20-year span this grew into an enormous body of work, and the collection of plates, drawings and texts provide genuinely worthwhile references in themselves.

My memories of the Historex workshop are of a place that was very calm, studious and serious, but also warm and friendly. The building had a windowed facade about 20 meters long, behind which were arranged a dozen tables in perpendicular rows where each engraver had his work space and drawers of tools. The Historex figures were the work of only one of these engravers, which explains the consistent style throughout the series. This engraver, Pierre Delhomme, was a grizzled old bachelor and an eccentric perfectionist who worked the hours he chose. He sometimes laboured through the night, on other occasions taking off for two or three days at a time - but he was an ace at his trade. In fact, our work led him to an interest in military uniforms which became an obsession. He enjoyed a unique position at the workshop which led to a certain jealousy on the part of the other engravers, whose work was less interesting. Delhomme and I passed many long evenings studying not only engraving but military history and costume.

Monsieur Gillet, the owner of Historex, was also interested in figures and did several dioramas based on my paintings; I did the settings and backgrounds. He was a nice man, if sometimes a little grumpy; very intelligent, and a master of his trade. It was at my house that he usually met people he wished to honour. Madame Gillet managed the office, at least in theory. In practice virtually all requests for information were sent to me to answer, and I must have answered thousands of them, one question often requiring a two-page response. I should have had a secretary!

The Historex competitions were always successful and enjoyable occasions. Unlike the shows today they were true celebrations of the figurine, and less a commercial event.

The end of the initial Historex venture [after René Gillet's death in 1985] was sad, with only a single engraver sitting without work amidst the silent machines. My son, who was the director during the final years, despaired alone in his office, without the money to develop new pieces for a dwindling clientele who seemed to have turned to new and different things.

But hope has been reborn with the new Historex firm; and I sincerely wish a successful rebirth to this venture, to which I have devoted so much of my heart and soul.

Eugéne Lelièpvre
Montrouge, France
August 1996

A Brief Company History: Lynn Sangster

I saw my first Historex figure in the winter of 1965, at one of the monthly meetings of the British Model Soldier Society. I purchased one as soon as possible, but it stood on the shelf for some time, looking rather wooden. I was at that time a devotee of Charles Stadden figures and was used to working in lead. However, while working in Paris in 1966 I visited an exhibition at the Maritime Museum in the Palais de Chaillot; and it was like seeing the light. An exhibition of Historex figures by Pierre Conrad, Eugéne Lelièpvre and René Gillet had been animated and altered in so many ways - dragoons leading their horses; hussar officers twisted in the saddle; soldiers holding their shakos and wiping their brows - these were figures that you could put into any position you wished. I was well and truly hooked.

At this period of my life I worked as a continental tour guide/courier, which meant six months at a time of 18-hour days, seven days a week, followed by six months' leave - a perfect arrangement for a dedicated modeller. I spent my six months' leave discovering the delights of Historex, acquiring Rousselot plates from the great man himself, and generally having a wonderful time. I also soon saw the commercial possibilities of introducing other UK model soldier enthusiasts to Historex figures. Historex was pleased to involve me as I could speak French, and no one working at Historex could speak English. This was the start of my

This diminutive 40mm Mokarex French Cuirassier foreshadows the movement and appeal of the later Historex horses. (Courtesy Dick Pielin)

own very happy relationship with Historex, which has continued for almost 30 years.

L'Atelier de Gravure, the engraving workshop, actually started making moulds for Historex kits in January 1963, and it is possible to tell when each figure mould was finished by the year/month numbering system used: for example, the moulds for 631 Revolutionary Hussars were made in January 1963, and 835 British Artillery Limbers in May 1983. Historex had its origins as an engraving studio founded in 1948 by a group of master engravers of whom René Gillet was a founding member. In 1955 a small manufacturing enterprise called Aeros began to make moulds and manufacture plastic aircraft kits. This was short-lived; however, at the same time the engravers had made figure moulds for a French coffee firm named Mokarex and a Belgian firm, Storme. These figures were given away with packets of coffee throughout both countries, and in the 1950s were very popular in modellers' collections. Actually, this was how as a young boy Jacques Vuyet of Le Cimier caught the figure "bug".

It was at this time that René Gillet was fortunate enough to make the acquaintance of

INTRODUCTION: THE HISTOREX STORY

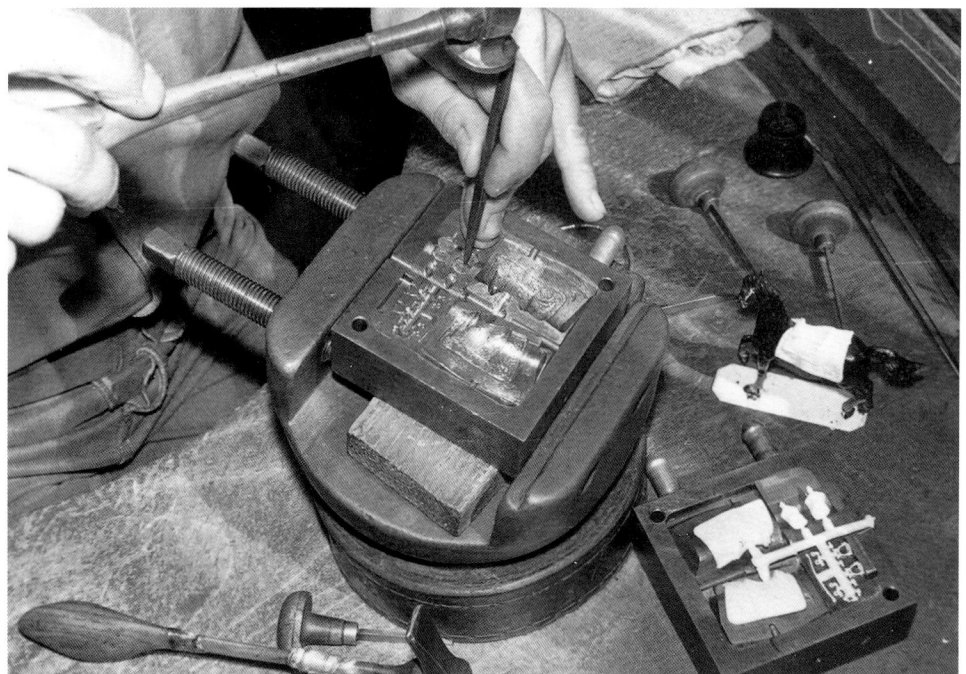

(Right) At one of the Historex workbenches, a moulding press is employed to produce horse halves from the completed moulds.

(Above and right) One of the Historex engravers creating an original figure mould in steel; and the engraving of a Historex saddle and accoutrements after checking and re-checking for fit and accuracy.

INTRODUCTION: THE HISTOREX STORY

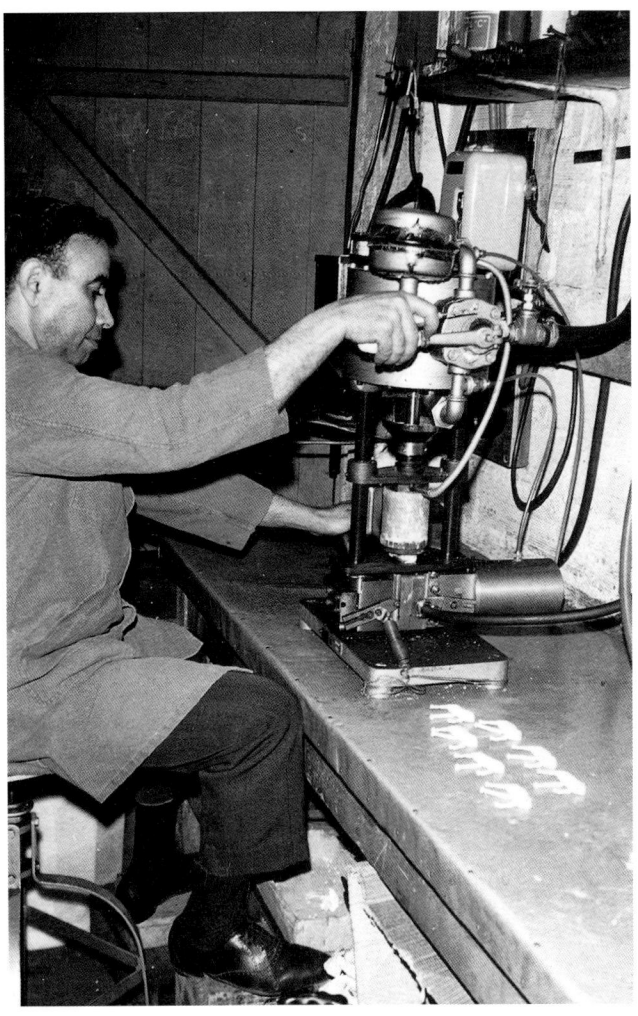

Eugéne Lelièpvre, an Official Painter to the French Army and an experienced figure maker with a vast knowledge of military uniforms and equestrian subjects. Gillet asked him to make the master figures and carry out all the research for Historex. The parts that Maitre Lelièpvre designed were then cut into small blocks of steel by engravers. These individuals spent 13 years proving themselves worthy to become master engravers, each beginning as an apprentice and graduating to become what was known as a *"petit ouvrier"*.

The manufacturing process involved white plastic being injected into the moulds, the plastic parts then being packed into a clear plastic bag with what has become a very distinctive orange header card. The first kits took a lot of courage on the part of Gillet and his partner, Monsieur Fualdes, to set the venture going. The high class figure market at that time was dominated by the traditional lead alloy soldier. Although plastic did not suffer from the oxidation (lead disease) which attacked metal figures, there was a widely held prejudice that plastic was a cheap modern medium suitable only for children's toys.

People tended to equate weight with quality: if it was heavy like gold, it must be valuable, and if it was light like plastic, it must be worthless!

To further complicate matters, the moulds were extraordinarily expensive to engrave; and the first mounted figure, according to René Gillet, cost up to £10,000 pounds to produce in 1963. This was an enormous sum in those days - ten times as much in today's values - and very difficult to recuperate. Admittedly, plastic was cheap to buy and produce; but the packing was a labour-intensive process, and accordingly expensive. Most plastic kits were made in large moulds and the entire kit ejected into a plastic bag and then into a box. With Historex kits, however, all of the parts were numbered, manufactured separately and sorted into bins. A packer armed with a list of numbers would then make up each kit. Thus the wonderful "spare parts" service became available to modellers; and what a boon that was!

One can still purchase individual heads, bodies, legs - in fact, nearly every part that Historex ever produced. This service must be unique in the world, and has always set Historex apart from other manufacturers. Without being too precise, it is estimated that there are over 1,500 spare part sprues, and each sprue averages ten different items; so there are 15,000 different parts, and over 1,000 different kits.

The name Historex was derived from the first five letters of the French word *histoire* and the last three letters from *Mokarex* - René Gillet thought French modellers and collectors would thus associate the name with figures. Quite surprisingly, Historex Aeros SA (the company's full name) never published a catalogue; it was left to the initiative of Historex Agents, their UK distributor, to do so. As a result, sales of Historex increased enormously wherever catalogues were sold. At this point one has to pay tribute to modellers such as Ray Lamb in England, who painted the marvellous Chasseur of the Guard figure, after the Géricault painting, which appeared on the first catalogue's cover - the figure still remains a standard to which many modellers aspire. In the USA Shep Paine used Historex in his wonderful dioramas and small vignettes, and in France Pierre Conrad painted very special pieces sought after by collectors and museums throughout the world.

I myself had excellent success with the sales of Historex in Great Britain, as we had a long history of model making unknown in many other countries. I once had the great satisfaction of reading in a German newspaper that "Sangster of Historex Agents had succeeded

INTRODUCTION: THE HISTOREX STORY

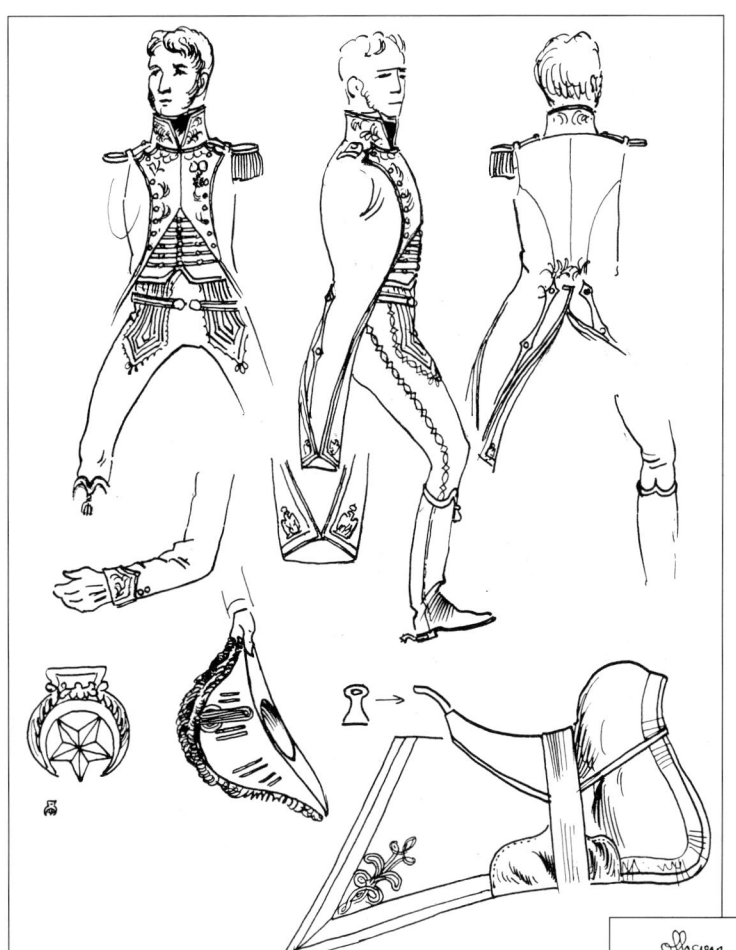

Sketches by Eugéne Lelièpvre for a senior officer figure, illustrating the amount of research which guaranteed both accuracy and fine detail in the finished figures.

(Below) Preliminary sketches of epaulettes and contre-epaulettes, collar and cuff details, sashes and tassels.

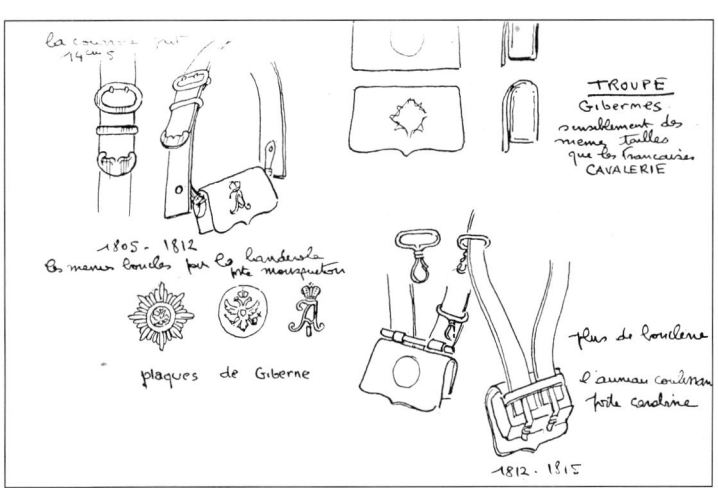

Maitre Lelièpvre's meticulous sketches for cartridge boxes, belts and buckles.

INTRODUCTION: THE HISTOREX STORY

A delightful Historex Tenth Anniversary sketch by Eugéne Lelièpvre.

where Napoleon failed, by placing large numbers of French troops on British soil".

Some modellers may also recall that the Atelier de Gravure made the moulds for a small series of World War II German figures together with weapons and field equipment, under the name of Armour Accessories. I well remember the occasion when Jerry Campbell of Squadron purchased 100,000 model jerrycans from me. When the consignment arrived in the States, however, the customs officials - not known for their sense of humour - were bemused by the description on the customs forms, typed by a secretary (who did not normally make mistakes) as "100,000 Amour Accessories"! . . . "What the heck do the French *do* with these?", one was heard to mutter.

The years between 1963 and 1985 were the great productive period for Historex. Gillet was the driving force, with his knowledge of engraving, and Maitre Lelièpvre lent his artistry to a very mechanical process. René Gillet was always full of ideas to advance the name of Historex, and started the Concours Historex - annual shows, held at Fontainbleau. The medals awarded were designed by an engraver friend who worked for Chaumet, the great Parisian jewellers, and lapel pins were given to traders and modellers in attendance.

Sadly, René Gillet died in July 1985, and with him the driving force behind the company. Production continued under Jacques Fualdes and Jacques Lelièpvre, but the very complexity of Historex production was commercially disastrous. Historex was producing so many different kits that shops could not afford to stock more than five per cent of the list, and retail sales dropped dramatically. At the same time many new manufacturers were emerging, and producing a wider range of kits in metal and resin covering many different historical periods. No new Historex moulds were produced due to ever-increasing production costs, and the company was eventually sold to Messieurs Treille and Pensec. There followed an even more difficult period and heavy financial losses. In 1991 Historex went into liquidation.

Offers were received by the liquidators from various parts of the globe, but the moulds and machinery were eventually purchased by Christian Sauvé and Associates. Happily, production continues today under the new name of NCO Historex and its sister producer, Nemrod. Today the cost of new moulds would

INTRODUCTION: THE HISTOREX STORY

be prohibitively high even if the expertise still existed to make them. Fortunately, the new resin parts perfectly match the plastic Historex parts. New figures and parts are now available, and indeed some of them are very exciting for Historex devotees. New heads, hands, legs, breeches, stockings and buckled shoes enable the modeller to convert figures into Society Dress as well as military uniforms, and there are other innovations.

Looking back, I genuinely believe that without Historex the model soldier world would not be in the same position it enjoys today. Manufacturers and modellers alike are producing miniature works of art, and I know from personal contact that many "cut their modelling teeth" on Historex. Looking forward, I still see a bright future for NCO Historex, both in the continuing production of plastic parts and the integration with new resin parts to make even more interesting pieces. I think this book by such a well-known exponent of Historex as Bill Ottinger will keep the Historex flame burning long into the future.

Lynn Sangster
Historex Agents
Dover, England
August 1996

**Historex kits and spares offer the combined pleasures of research, assembly, painting and collecting in one of the most colourful and dramatic periods of military history.
(Courtesy Nick Infield)**

INTRODUCTION: THE HISTOREX STORY

CHAPTER ONE
THE FIGURE LINE

What do you want to create? Napoleon and his Marshals? A tattered Grenadier of the Guard? A British Light Dragoon? A mounted Highlander officer? A Mameluke? Or Napoleon mounted on Marengo? The range of Historex kits borders on the astounding, including figures which can be mixed and matched to produce officers, enlisted men, trumpeters, musicians, and virtually any combat or support arm of the Napoleonic period. In addition, the range of Historex accessories supplies anything from eating utensils, to a covered British shako, to a pontoon bridge.

The Historex line was an innovation which allowed modellers this tremendous versatility for the first time. All parts were interchangeable which, in turn, meant that every piece had to be in a constant scale. The process was lengthy and much more involved than accepted mass production methods. Every limb, weapon, decoration, saddle, or epaulette was researched in exhaustive detail. A lead master figure was then produced, corrected and recorrected; and an epoxy-cast mould was made of the individual pieces. Test figures were next produced in plastic; and when accuracy was assured, the final steel moulds were engraved to perfection by hand.

While British, Prussian, Russian, and other armies of the period can be recreated, the French Napoleonic army has dominated the line. The period 1730-63 in French history has also received attention, while a few recent releases include post-Napoleonic figures. Recent additions have been supplemented by the new Nemrod line of figures produced by NCO Historex, which incorporate earlier Historex parts with these new resin figures.

Historex also produce a series of prepackaged vignettes entitled the Living Model Series, containing figures and accessories to create scenes such as "The Battery of Fearless Men", "The Relay Courier", "The Dance of the Sabres", and 25 other groupings. There are also detailed models of French and British artillery teams; these can be built to stand by themselves, or to include artillerymen, drivers, etc. A field forge, a medical wagon, a vivandiére's cart, and an ambulance are also available. Dogs, saddlebags, sporrans, bagpipes, baskets, clogs, donkeys, tigerskin shabraques, and a choice of Germanic-style tobacco pipes give only a glimpse of the variety of parts which can be purchased separately.

As examples of the variety and conversion possibilities, there are 39 pairs of arms alone. There are numerous seated, standing and riding legs, torsos and coattails. Heads include generic faces with varying period hairstyles, as well as portrait heads for such notables as Napoleon, Murat, Ney, Roustam, Lannes, and a host of other recognizable figures of the period. The list has been supplemented by the recent additions from Nemrod; the new resin heads are superb additions to the line, especially the negroid heads and those with different facial expressions.

As an example of the number of parts offered, Shep Paine related an early experience when he was converting a French cavalryman to a mounted Scots Grey (prior to the release of the kit). After ordering a plain leather sabretache from Lynn Sangster at Historex Agents, he received the wrong one. When he called to get the correct part, Lynn informed him that Historex did not make one. When he checked with Historex they agreed that the part was not available. Shep pointed out that an existing kit indeed included that particular part: such was the sheer number of parts that even the manufacturer and distributor ultimately lost track of what was available!

The list of specialty parts is far too numerous to list separately. This includes, for example, 26 different French swords (plus two sapper's axes), six French muskets and various bayonets. These are supplemented by various Allied weapons, plus pennants, guidons, lances, haversacks, insignia, cuffs, collars,

CHAPTER ONE: THE FIGURE LINE

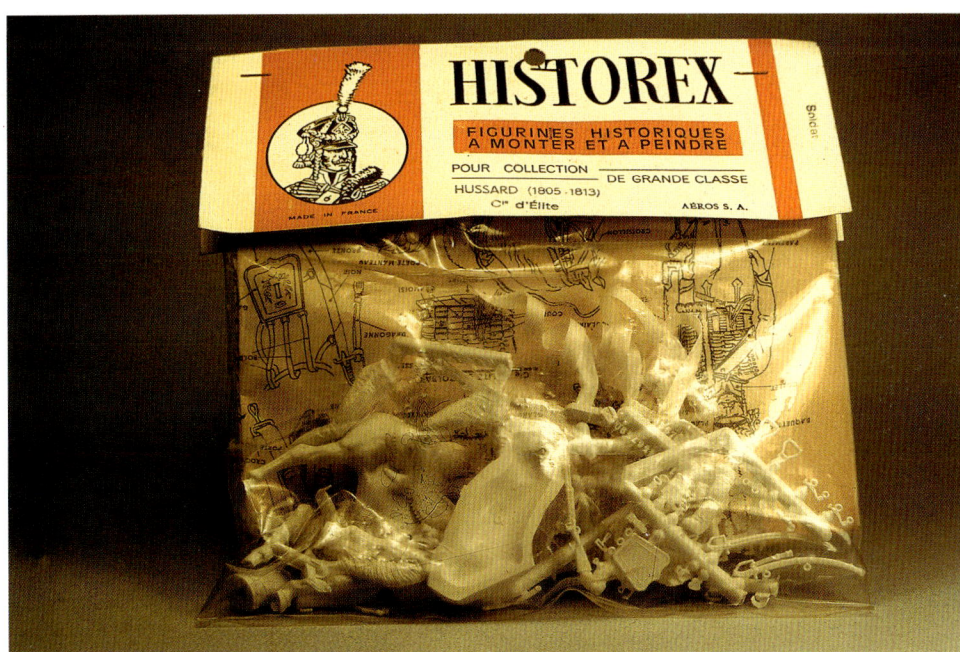

(Left) The early Historex package contained a wonderful but sometimes perplexing jumble of detailed parts.

boots, bicornes, turbans, and countless other small items to replicate original equipment.

One of the most appealing features of Historex is the amount of detail present in each figure. This is enhanced by the fact that most parts are moulded separately instead of being cast onto the figure, as is usually the case with their white metal counterparts. While some painters may view this as demanding extra work, the final results more than make up for the time expended. The pure quantity of detail that can be incorporated into a single figure renders them not only accurate, but unique.

Constant scale

The availability of so many parts is enhanced by the consistency of scale, which is constant almost without exception. Although listed as 54mm (1/32), Historex figures actually measure closer to 56-58mm (1/30) scale. This may seem an insignificant difference except when attempting to incorporate non-scale items, when Historex product will appear noticeably larger than most standard 1/32 and 1/35 scale parts. Mixing parts from other manufacturers with Historex components usually does not work. A few inconsistencies may be tolerable or negligible on a completed figure, but inaccurate anatomical proportions or undersized equipment will visibly spoil the entire effect.

Making the most of all the detail and accuracy of a completed Historex figure demands a combination of modelling skills with painting ability. Make no mistake: a real modelling effort is required to produce one of these gems to its true level of potential. I can still remember admiring photos of Historex figures by painters such as Max Longhurst, Ray Lamb, Shep Paine and Graham Bickerton; and I can also remember the apprehension I felt when I received my first Historex kit through the mail - how was I supposed to get from Point A to Point B?

Opening that little bag of white plastic parts dulled my enthusiasm for only a few moments. Any apprehension was overcome by my admiration as I recognized the detail and accuracy evident in the mass of small pieces; and what the heck, I had built untold aircraft kits, hadn't I? Besides, my growing interest in Napoleonic cavalry left me few other options if I wanted to reproduce a variety of subjects beyond the castings then available on the market. But before I delved into that first kit, it became obvious that I would need to up-grade my reference material.

Collecting references

While the uniform descriptions which came with the kit were excellent, the assembly instructions were bare bones, to say the least. A colourful but small Lelièpvre uniform card was included, but this did not show complete detail from all angles. Inside the package were black and white illustrations of the figure, and a very good written outline of the figure's various uniforms (enlisted man, officer, trumpeter); but no identification of the individual parts, nor any instructions as to exactly how they were to be assembled. Today's Historex

CHAPTER ONE: THE FIGURE LINE

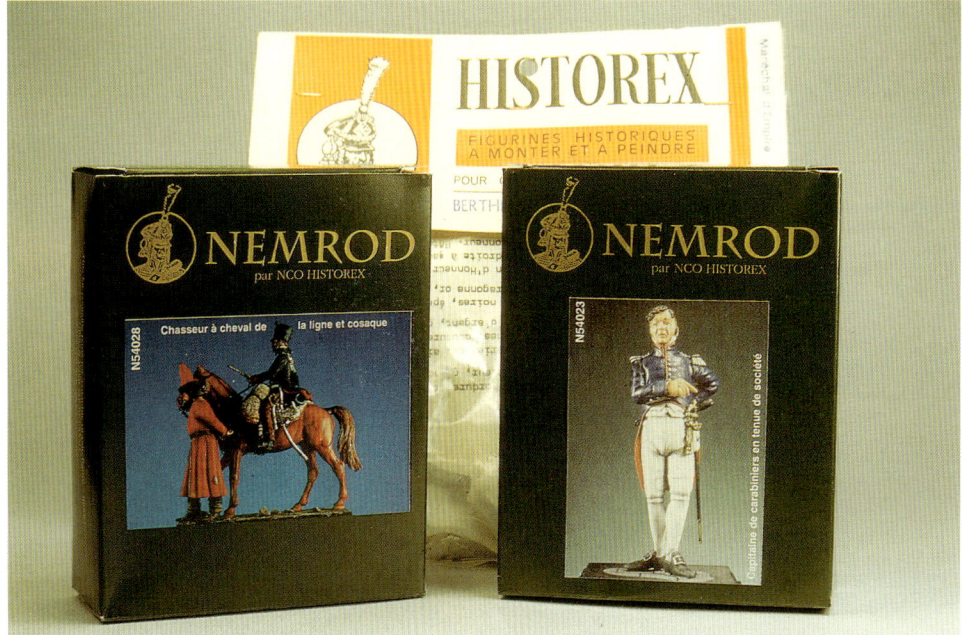

(Left & below) After the death of M.René Gillet and the tragic failure of the original business the Historex range were saved - to the relief of modellers everywhere - and have now been augmented by new releases from Nemrod, part of the current NCO Historex ownership under the auspices of Christian Sauvé.

kits contain more information and up-dated instructions.

Over the years I acquired a suitable array of information and references, including the Rousselot and Rigo uniform plates, Osprey books, and other sources for Napoleonic uniform details. The Historex Agents catalogues were themselves especially useful for basic reference. The earlier ones (hard to locate now, but worth the effort) are full of good colour photos, "how to" articles, illustrations, diorama tips, and articles on painting horses by Eugéne Lelièpvre. Today's catalogues and spare parts lists have additional information, including samples of basic Napoleonic uniform colours.

I came to realize that my reference library was focused on uniforms and equipment. Creating human body parts or modifying a horse was something entirely new for an aircraft modeller. I had to learn some rudimentary basics about both forms. There was no need to become an aspiring surgeon (plastic surgeon?!) or veterinarian, but I did need to acquire a working knowledge to avoid producing freaks of nature. Just as an aircraft or armour modeller knows that creating an accurate model demands accuracy of scale, outline and details, so the figure modeller has to educate the eye to judge the accuracy of representations of humans and horses: an arm that looks as if it were made of rubber, or a horse's leg in an impossible position, wastes all the hours of effort invested in the details.

Once I felt that I had the basic reference material, the next step was to dive into the bag of parts. This is where my former experience with plastic aircraft kits proved useful. For anyone with past experience in plastic modelling of any sort, building Historex figures will not be as intimidating as it may first appear. In fact, given the new photo-etched parts and

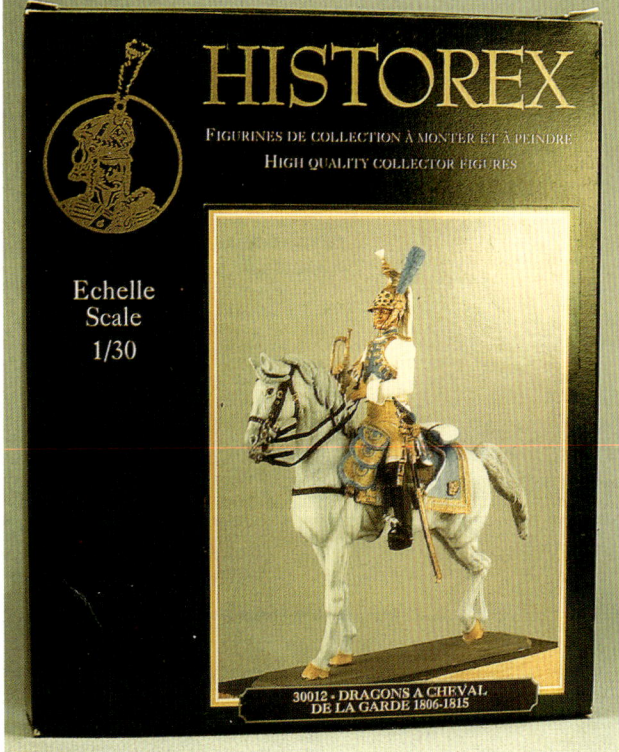

(Opposite) The standard against which so many subsequent Historex figures and conversions were compared: Ray Lamb's beautifully rendered "Officer of the Chasseurs of the Guard", which appeared in the Historex Agents catalogue - now itself a collector's item.

CHAPTER ONE: THE FIGURE LINE

Shep Paine, USA:

Detail from Shep Paine's "The King of Rome". (Photo Lane Stewart)

"I bought my first Historex figure at the battlefield of Waterloo. At that time I had the usual experience with plastic models and a casual acquaintance with metal figure kits, so the idea of doing plastic figures struck a chord with me from the outset.

"I did most of my Historex figures (close to a hundred of them) in the years 1968 to 1976. To some extent they were the 'training wheels on my bicycle', providing the necessary background in anatomy and detail for later work in free-form sculpture. But that does not mean that I am not still pleased with my Historex figures, or that I dismiss them as 'apprentice work'. I have had occasion to see these pieces again over the years, and while I certainly would change some things, on the whole I can look back with satisfaction on the work that they represent.

"Like most people, I was first attracted by the fine detail, but it did not take long for me to realize that the conversion potential was the real value of these figures. The styrene plastic was a lot easier to cut, carve and convert than lead alloy, and the anatomical stiffness inherent in interchangeable parts was easily overcome if one knew where to cut and paste. More importantly, I soon came to value the freedom of posing that the light weight of the material afforded. Dramatic action poses which in metal would have collapsed under their own weight proved to be quite sturdy in styrene, provided they were reinforced with a bit of wire. It soon became a challenge to see how far the medium could be pushed, and the last few pieces I did involved figures seemingly posed in mid-air (the most dramatic probably being the two Highlanders in 'Scotland Forever' and the jumping horse suspended from the rider's foot in 'Roman Riding').

"I had long been fascinated by Napoleon's empire, and these figures furthered my interest in historical research, which quickly led me to the Rousselot plates. I was delighted to find in Historex a way to bring M.Rousselot's beautifully detailed illustrations to three-dimensional form, and by constantly discovering that the parts I found in the kit perfectly matched the drawings. Since that time I have acquired a number of original period weapons and uniform items, and am always amazed at how faithfully the Historex parts reproduce them.

"My most ambitious Historex project was the 'Eve of Essling', which drew its inspiration from several Meissonier renditions of Napoleon and his staff. I was attracted not so much by the splendour of the assembled uniforms as by the natural poses Meissonier had devised for his figures. I chose the subject of Essling not because it was a significant battle, but because it was the only one where all of the personalities I wanted to portray were present. By Waterloo many of the best-known personalities were dead, and at earlier battles one or more of the major characters always seemed to be on detached duty. I soon discovered that the secret of doing a large scene like this was to assemble it from several smaller vignettes, so that it does not look like a formal group photograph. I wasn't entirely sure that I could finish a project this large, so I did all of the figures separately, and then assembled them together to form the final scene.

"If I had to pick a personal favourite among my Historex pieces, it might be 'The King of Rome'. This is based on a story from the memoirs of Captain Coignet of the Imperial Guard. As a sergeant on pass one Sunday, he was walking through the Tuileries gardens when he was approached by an officer of the court and asked if he would mind carrying the Emperor's son for a few minutes, as the lady presently given the honour was getting tired. He reluctantly agreed, and found himself - a grizzled old bachelor terrified of babies - carrying the most precious infant in all of Europe. The child paid no attention to him, but proceeded to yank the plume from his bearskin and pull all the feathers from it.

"At the time the model was done no one was doing extensive conversions, which the baby would clearly require. The long gown would hide most of the child's anatomy, but I knew that I couldn't sculpt a baby's face. Inspiration struck me when I realized that I could carve down the head of Josephine from the Historex coronation set into a fair approximation of a baby's head. I think perhaps the irony of the King of Rome starting out as Josephine (whom Napoleon divorced because she couldn't produce an heir) is what makes me look back on this project so fondly.

"Another piece I look back on with pleasure is 'Wetting Down the Stripes', which was also inspired by Coignet's memoirs. What hit me was that my friends and I had celebrated with the very same ritual my own promotion to sergeant in the US Army 160 years later!"

(Right) The series of beautiful uniform plates by Lucien Rousselot continue to be the most accurate and detailed reference available. Virtually every Historex part can be identified by careful comparison with these plates.

CHAPTER ONE: THE FIGURE LINE

minute plastic detail now included in aircraft and armour kits, Historex should pose no problems for the serious modeller.

The only inhibiting factor to experimenting with Historex figures is the amount of time and effort one is willing to devote to each project. Personally, I am willing to reduce my total output in order to create certain figures which intrigue me. Since I am not under any time constraints, I can work as much detail as I want into each figure. I like the idea of producing a unique miniature and knowing that there will not be fifty others just like it; and the line's versatility lets me produce a thoroughly individual figure of virtually any Napoleonic subject.

Another attractive feature is Historex's flexibility. Greg DiFranco, an excellent Historex modeller and painter, made a very accurate observation when he said that Historex was more of a medium than a kit. The combination of parts, subjects and easily worked polystyrene present the modeller with a very versatile medium to create new variations of

(Right) Kerry Ready's "6th Hussar, 1796", another early example of the inherent movement and detail possible with Historex kits.

CHAPTER ONE: THE FIGURE LINE

The author's "Carabinier Officer" by Nemrod, which includes a Historex helmet and horse; note the excellent Nemrod cape, and the period tobacco pipe from the Historex spares range.

Napoleonic figures. For me it meant that I could indulge in extensive construction and painting, both of which are appealing to me, and there were unlimited conversion possibilities. This meant that I could create a mood, an impression of a type of motion, or a "story" without compromising accuracy or my wallet. Combining the skills acquired from earlier plastic models with whatever painting abilities I learned opened up a whole world of new possibilities.

Like most manufacturers, Historex has its weaknesses, but none are fatal; the majority of small flaws are due to production limitations. The company's ability to produce accurate detail more than compensates for the few areas that need additional work. As the reader goes through the chapters on assembling and converting figures these areas will be covered in detail, along with advice on how to make both major and minor changes.

CHAPTER ONE: THE FIGURE LINE

(Left) An early vignette by Shep Paine entitled "The Forager", depicting a French hussar whose booty seems to include most of the essential food groups...

(Right) A nicely weathered French ambulance by Larry Munné, including a medical orderly and a surgeon complete with his case of instruments.

(Left) An early example of the excellent work by a Historex pioneer, Pierre Conrad, using standard Carabinier kits.

(Left) Currently one of Italy's best Historex modellers and painters is Ivo Preda. His "Dragoon Kettledrummer of the Imperial Guard" is primarily a Historex kit with a Segom head and some scratchbuilding.

(Right) A colourful example of the never-ending array of splendid uniforms worn by French Napoleonic trumpeters. The author's "Trumpeter, 9th Hussars" illustrates the amount of movement which can be incorporated into horse and rider.

CHAPTER ONE: THE FIGURE LINE

(Left) The light weight and relative strength of Historex's styrene material allows dramatic animations of extreme movement - the author's "Trooper, 5th Chasseurs à Cheval" is supported by a single hoof touching the groundwork. Note also the individual details which can be added, such as the bandaged leg and unbuttoned overall cuff.

(Right) Confronted by the work of a master, it is often difficult to imagine how so much fine detail can be included in a small scale model. Claudio Signanini of Italy amply shows what careful painting can accomplish in this "Hussar Officer, 1807". Remember that the actual model is smaller than its reproduction on this page.

(Below) "The Wounded Drummer Boy" by Dave Peschke, an excellent example of the focusing of attention so important in multiple-figure vignettes.

(Right) "Eugéne de Beauharnais, 1806" by Ivo Preda, with superb painting of the sabretache details, pelisse lace and horse. The rider is a rebuilt Le Cimier figure.

CHAPTER TWO
ASSEMBLY, DETAILING & ENHANCEMENT

The most daunting moment for a newcomer to the Historex line is the first sight of all those little white plastic parts. My first approach is to open the bag and carefully inspect all the parts. Examine them, but don't separate them from the sprue trees yet; you only want to become familiar with them at this point, fixing in your mind exactly what they are. If you cannot immediately identify all parts, do a little research - they may be spares for another kit, or they may not even apply to the figure you've selected! Like some other kit manufacturers, Historex provide spare parts, and some kit parts overlap. If you simply cannot identify it, forget it and forge ahead. It'll either identify itself as and when you need it, or else it cannot be that crucial to the final figure.

The more Historex figures you build, the more you'll become familiar with the parts and uniforms; sooner or later you'll be able to identify everything on sight. The Rousselot plates are invaluable for the serious Napoleonic painter and offer a wealth of uniform, equipment and horse furniture detail. In fact, you will eventually realize that every Historex part can be identified using these plates.

There are two methods to approaching Historex kits. Some modellers open each kit and separate the parts into labelled containers or drawers; others keep the kits together. I generally fall into the latter camp, but I also have a very large supply of spare parts culled from kits or purchased separately. Sometimes I use the kit, sometimes I build the figure entirely from spare parts - it depends on the subject matter. Purchase several small chests with clear plastic drawers into which parts can be separated and labelled for future use; your local hardware or craft store will stock them.

Tools and materials

The tools needed to build and convert Historex are not extensive. Besides a few exotic ones which are easily obtained, you probably have most of them already:

(Left) Three contrasting uniforms of the earliest Napoleonic period - a Grenadier, a Hussar and a Fusilier - portrayed by Edward Pollard. The horse's tail has been replaced with crepe hair, a popular touch of super-detailing.

(Right & over) The author's "Murat, King of Naples" incorporates more than 200 individual parts - a good example of the complexity of assembly of many Historex figures. The red and blue sashes, the cuffs and the epaulette fringe were all added with A+B epoxy putty; the Légion d'Honneur decoration is supplied by Historex.

CHAPTER TWO: ASSEMBLY, DETAILING & ENHANCEMENT

Micro files
Hobby files
Flat "bastard" file
Flexigrit sandpaper
Sanding sticks (Squadron Shop)
Razor saw
No.11 Xacto blades (buy them in bulk)
Sharp dental picks, and root canal files (ask your dentist for old ones)
Small pliers
"Third hand" tool
Small pair of dividers
Hemostat
Insect pins
Shirt pins
Various brass rods and wire
Lead wire of various gauges (from fly fishing shops)
Pin vice
Dremel or other good miniature electric drill with rheostat (transformer) and speed control, or Dremel Mini-Mite
Pyrogravure with temperature control or rheostat/transformer

A+B epoxy putty (white, if possible), available in UK as Sylmasta A+B - see Note on Suppliers; or equivalent product Milliput, readily available in UK
Duro epoxy putty ribbon, available in UK as Kneadatite Duro (see Note on Suppliers)
Duro Five Minute epoxy or other two-part epoxy cement
Super-glue (my favourite in the USA is Crazy Glue)
Testors or other good liquid plastic cement
Liquid sprue (homemade - see below)

I also like to make some of my own tools. For example, an insect pin inserted and glued into a small dowel is an excellent all-purpose tool. Small strips of Flexigrit sandpaper glued onto toothpicks and small dowels (curved and flattened) are great for sanding hard-to-reach spots. Sharpened round toothpicks also work well for adding creases and folds; carve the tip into the diameter you prefer, sand the tip smooth and strengthen it with several coats of Crazy Glue for a smoother surface. Insofar as No.11 Xacto blades are concerned, buy them in bulk packages. Very sharp blades are a necessity, so don't hesitate to change blades as often as you want during construction - 15 to 20 can be used during the making of a single mounted figure.

The pyrogravure is basically a hot knife with a finely sharpened tip instead of a knife blade. Its value lies in its ability to texture plastic surfaces, and to remove wedges of plastic when converting parts. Most of them are sold with a somewhat blunt tip which needs to be filed down to a much finer point. The alternative is to convert a soldering iron by replacing the tip with a length of brass wire sharpened to a needle point. I've used both with the same results. Simulating the fur of headgear, sheepskin saddle covers, pelisses, etc. is easy once you master its use. Just remember that the tip and heating barrel get **very** hot, and the fumes are toxic, so use it only in a well-ventilated area. By attaching it to a rheostat (transformer) the heat can be controlled to produce various results. Be **very** careful: it's painfully easy to burn yourself, or - even worse - ruin the figure. The same applies to the speed setting on an electric drill/cutting tool: keep it slow, or friction heat can melt hours of work into a sticky blob before your eyes.

The "third hand" tool is available from several manufacturers; it's basically a heavy stand with two alligator clips which can hold a figure or parts firmly, allowing you to use both hands to attach delicate parts or paint hard-to-reach areas. Be certain to wrap masking tape around the clips to prevent marring the figure's surface. This tool is also especially useful if you're painting a horse posed on one leg; it allows repeated handling of the horse, which would otherwise be vulnerable to breakage if temporarily attached at a single point.

CHAPTER TWO: ASSEMBLY, DETAILING & ENHANCEMENT

Clean-up

The first step, as in any type of modelling, is to remove the mould lines and any blemishes left by the sprue at the point of attachment. It's an easy task to scrape off these seam lines using the sharp side of a No.11 blade placed at a right angle to the plastic; sand away whatever remains. Be careful not to remove moulded-on detail. Look also for small parts that can be enhanced by reducing their thickness, e.g. buckles, epaulettes, medals, bridle hardware, etc. are generally too thick due to moulding restrictions. The easiest way to correct this is to hold the part against a flat sheet of Flexigrit or fine sandpaper, sanding the back of the part beneath your fingertip. The thickness of sword blades also needs to be reduced to proper scale by gently scraping both sides with a new No.11 blade. Polish the reduced surfaces with very fine sandpaper before painting.

As in most endeavours, you'll be rewarded by the results of such additional work. The several nights you may spend cleaning up the dozens of parts for a complex mounted figure will be repaid many times over when you begin painting. Sharpening division lines, careful undercutting, fitting, filling, etc., is always worth the time invested; don't be impatient - you aren't under a deadline.

WORKING WITH THE FIGURE

There are many approaches to building, improving and converting Historex and other plastic figures. What follows may seem complex at first glance; but the amount of time expended on each figure can vary tremendously from modeller to modeller. Much depends upon individual preferences, or whether the figure is intended for competition.

Building Historex figures always presents an initial quandary for the modeller. There's all that beautiful detail waiting to be assembled. At the same time there's a realization that any figure can be improved, especially if the medium is easy to work. Historex's styrene material lends itself to alterations; cutting, sawing, melting, snipping, heating, drilling and pinning take little effort. Even a disastrous mistake can be corrected without huge expenditure. Success, however, requires that the modeller must learn a few basics about human and equine anatomy; even the best painting cannot cover flawed anatomy, and the smallest mistake is magnified if elementary rules are violated.

(Above) The author's "Officer, Grenadiers of the Guard" is a much simpler project, assembled from standard Historex parts with only a few additional modifications.

You don't need daunting and expensive medical tomes - the most accessible sources for this sort of reference are basic figure drawing primers, found in most art supply shops and the arts and crafts sections of bookshops. There are many lines available, with titles such as *How to Draw the Human Figure*, *How to Draw Horses*, etc; most are inexpensive, with large, clear instructional drawings which build up the basic body masses and their movements. As already mentioned, I don't plan to repeat here the basic methods of model conversion already extensively covered elsewhere; but I can recommend two books without reservations, both of which include chapters which are applicable to Historex work: Shep Paine's *Building and Painting Scale Figures* (Kalmbach, 1993); and Bill Horan's *Military*

CHAPTER TWO: ASSEMBLY, DETAILING & ENHANCEMENT

(Above) This "Line Lancer" by Pierre Conrad is a straight forward assembly with few, if any, changes from the basic kit.

The other leg can remain unchanged. Next, tilt the figure's body and hips slightly downward towards the leg supporting the figure's weight. Rather than belabouring this point or trying to improve upon Shep Paine's description of this procedure, I refer the reader to his book on figures (see above).

Cementing and pinning

Three glues work best for assembly. Liquid plastic cement is a must, even in today's era of cyanoacrylate super-glues. The strongest bond results from applying liquid plastic cement to both parts. Super-glues are great for quick attachments, but be careful: you cannot shift the part once the glue sets, and if precise location is critical then liquid plastic cement is a better alternative, giving additional time to position the part. The third glue is epoxy cement, which comes in two tubes and is mixed in equal parts. The bond is very strong and especially useful where non-plastic parts are used (for example, gluing a brass rod into a horse's leg or into a hole in the base), or where extra time is needed to position parts. However, it makes a relatively bulky mass of "treacle", and must be used with restraint.

The most basic plastic modeller's rule of all is not to use too much cement, or it will melt small parts to destruction and leak unattractively out of the joins between bigger items - the shameful badge of the impatient novice. Apply cements sparingly, with the tip of a pin or a small paintbrush. One obvious tip: remember to remove any paint from prepainted surfaces to be joined by any type of glue - otherwise you are simply attaching paint to paint, which is a uselessly weak bond.

One tricky aspect of handling Historex parts is their diminutive size. How do you handle the smallest parts, especially when gluing them into place? The easiest method is to pick them up on the tip of a new No.11 blade and then add a dot of glue to the part you are manipulating. If the part is extremely small you can forego the rule of applying liquid cement to both surfaces, since too much glue can simply dissolve the smaller part, and as smaller parts bear no weight permanent bonding presents no problem. An alternative for manipulating tiny parts is simply to pick them up on the wetted tip of a paintbrush.

The use of pins also eases assembly in many situations; in fact, I don't think I could build Historex figures without them. Two types are most useful, starting with the common shirt pin. These are normally used for extra strengthening of joins and initial positioning of

Modelling Masterclass (Windrow & Greene, 1994).

A stock Historex figure built "straight out of the package" will be accurate but somewhat stiff. Few people in real life stand with their weight evenly distributed on both feet, or sit ramrod straight. Changing the stance of a foot figure, a rider's position in the saddle, or head posture is relatively simple but very effective. This book deals almost exclusively with mounted figures; however, foot figures require some work to reduce their unnatural stiffness.

There are four steps which can correct this appearance. First, open out the hips by inserting a small shim of plastic at the front of the pelvis. Next, move one leg under the body until it is directly in line with the figure's spine. This is the leg that supports the body's weight in a casual stance; it should be straight, or modified to bend slightly backwards, i.e with the knee locked and the calf bowing out a little.

CHAPTER TWO: ASSEMBLY, DETAILING & ENHANCEMENT

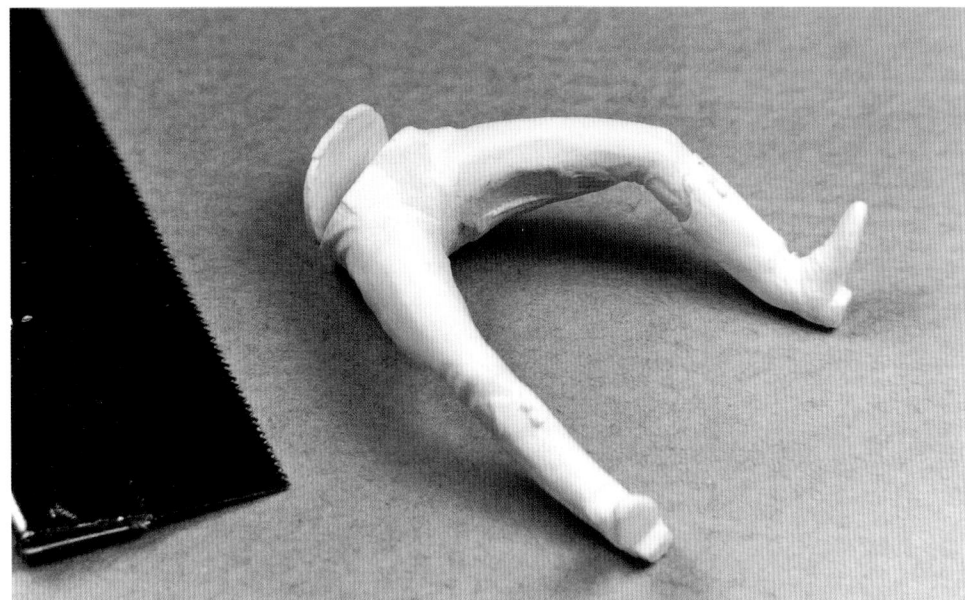

(Left) Using a razor saw, remove approximately 1/16in from the top of the assembled legs to correct the rider's height.

(Right) The torso selected for the mounted "Trumpeter, 20th Chasseurs à Cheval" is cemented to the legs with an overlap to accomodate the coattails.

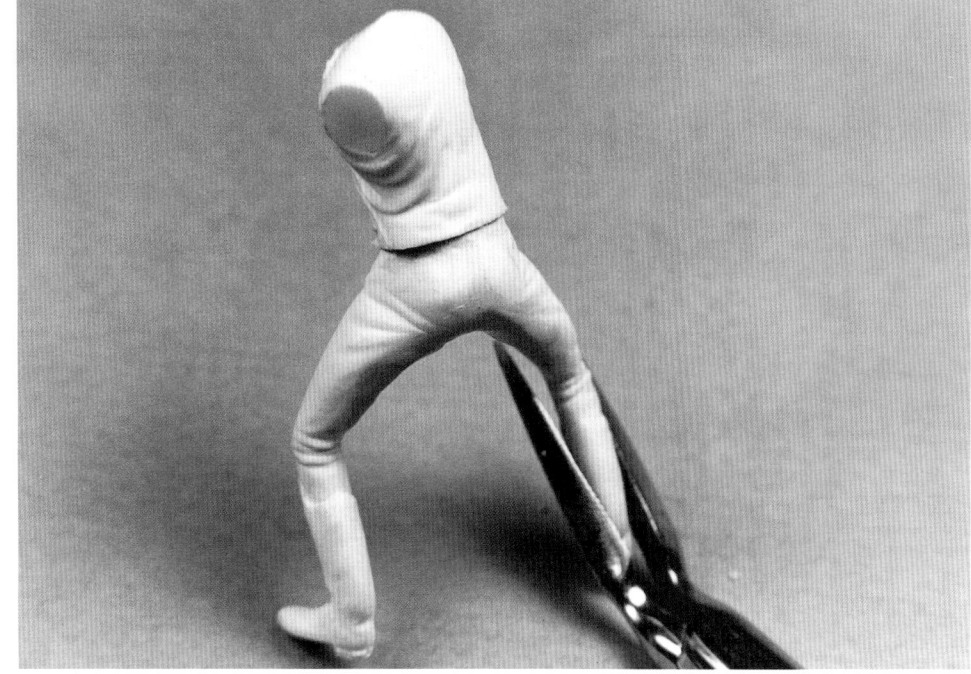

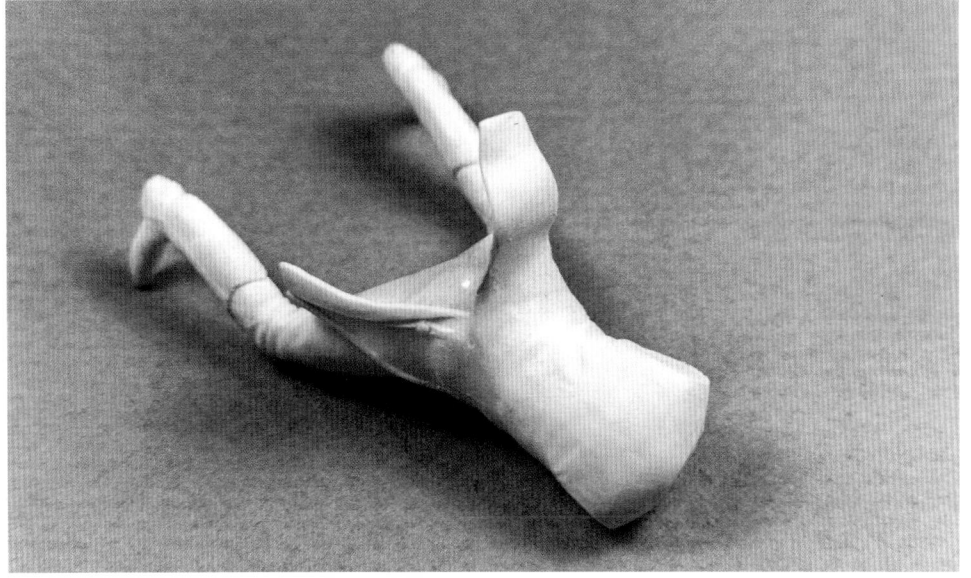

(Left) The coattails are faired into the overlapping bottom edge of the torso using A+B putty. A new left coattail had to be created from A+B to fit snugly over the valise behind the saddle once the figure was mounted.

CHAPTER TWO: ASSEMBLY, DETAILING & ENHANCEMENT

parts, especially if you are repositioning parts in extreme ways which will later require extensive filling. Insect pins are almost indispensable for smaller parts which require a strong attachment point. For example, attaching a plume to the top of a shako is easy when you use a short length of insect pin inserted into holes in the plume and shako drilled out by small root canal files.

These "drill bits" are actually minute files, extremely strong and endlessly useful. The small plastic handle can be broken off with pliers, leaving a very versatile bit. The tiny drill bits sold in hobby shops are extremely brittle and less reliable, so ask your dentist to save a few of these unpleasant but useful files for you rather than throwing them out after use.

"Liquid sprue" or "soup" is another useful resource. This is made simply by dropping small cut-up scraps of Historex plastic from the kit sprues into a partly used bottle of liquid plastic cement, where they will dissolve until you achieve the viscous liquid consistency you want; then close the bottle tightly. "Painted" on to the model, this goop solidifies in a thin film which can be progressively built up as needed; it is handy for adding fur or other areas to be worked up with a pyrogravure. It is best applied slowly in small increments, using a toothpick; let it dry thoroughly before working the new surface with the pyrogravure.

(**Safety note:** All solvents, i.e. liquid cements and super-glues, are dangerous if inhaled, and also highly volatile and inflammable - do NOT smoke near open containers, which should be kept closed when not in actual use. The fumes which are given off when plastic is melted are TOXIC; be careful not to inhale them, and always be sure to work in a well-ventilated area.)

Hands, heads and other details

Hands are an important detail of any figure, often being highly noticeable. Unfortunately, however, they are one of Historex's weak points: except for the opened hands and the

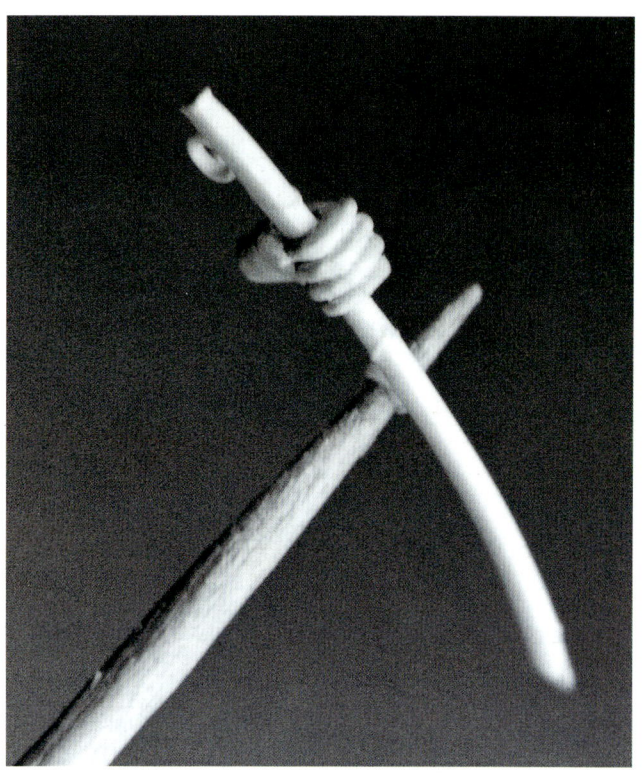

(Top) New hands were sculpted in lifelike positions, grasping the scabbard and the sabre. The hands were inserted into the drilled-out sleeve sockets much later in the assembly process.

(Right) The author's "ADC to General Rapp"; this pose illustrates the importance of carefully aligning the head, in this case to aim a pistol.

CHAPTER TWO: ASSEMBLY, DETAILING & ENHANCEMENT

(Left) At this stage the negroid head proper to this trumpeter has been attached, positioned facing towards some oncoming danger, and the figure has been modified into the position of drawing his sabre from the scabbard. Note the new collar opening, to match the altered angle of the head, and the sleeve sockets drilled for the hands.

newer resin hands, most are poorly designed and moulded. The time necessary to repair this weakness is worthwhile, since the viewer's eye is inevitably drawn to whatever the hands are doing or holding. Too often one sees hands which are supposedly grasping a weapon but which are revealed by a close look to be holding it by magnetism! The fingers either don't wrap around the object, or they are represented by blobs of putty with painted lines inadequately indicating fingers.

My preference is first to remove the existing hand from the arm. This allows me to position the hand later without it interfering with painting. For the corrections discussed below, this process is the easiest. A length of pin or stiff wire is inserted into the wrist, providing a temporary handle and an armature for sculpting a new wrist. Any excess length can be snipped off when fitting the hand to the arm.

To begin, file the end of the sleeve flat. Drill out about 1/4 inch of the end of the sleeve to accommodate the wrist when it is later attached. Drilling out the sleeve is easy if you acquire some used dental burrs (rounded drill bits) from your dentist.

There are four methods to improve the hands, depending upon the action being depicted. If the hand is not gripping an object, completely separating the fingers greatly improves their overall appearance. To accomplish this use the back edge of a No. 11 blade, lightly scraping between the fingers with repetitive strokes.

If the hands are grasping an object, use one of the following methods to correct the problem. First, you can replace the hand with another manufacturer's part. Locating a suitable hand may be difficult, however, since the Historex 1/30 scale does not easily match up with other scales. The closest match are Airfix's 1/32 Multi-Pose hands, but you have to purchase an entire box of figures to get the hands! There are many 1/35 scale hands but most are far too small in relation to Historex. You may be able to use the Historex drummers' hands, but they do not always grip in the right manner, and can appear too small. The third option is to gently heat the Historex hands. They can be held against a 100 watt light bulb for 15-20 seconds and then be bent carefully around the grasped object. I've used this method successfully, but I believe the final alternative gives better results.

After selecting the most appropriate Historex hand, remove all of the fingers and thumb. Rework the palm to accommodate whatever object is being held, and then glue it directly to the object. Sculpt new fingers and a thumb around whatever is being held; begin by first rolling out small "logs" of A+B putty, fairing them onto the hand and wrapping them around the object. Look carefully at your own hand and observe that the fingers are not spaghetti-like, but are jointed to form angles; also observe how the fingers are positioned in relation to the thumb. Don't forget to add knuckles, using a small wet brush to smooth out the putty.

The good news is that NCO Historex are

CHAPTER TWO: ASSEMBLY, DETAILING & ENHANCEMENT

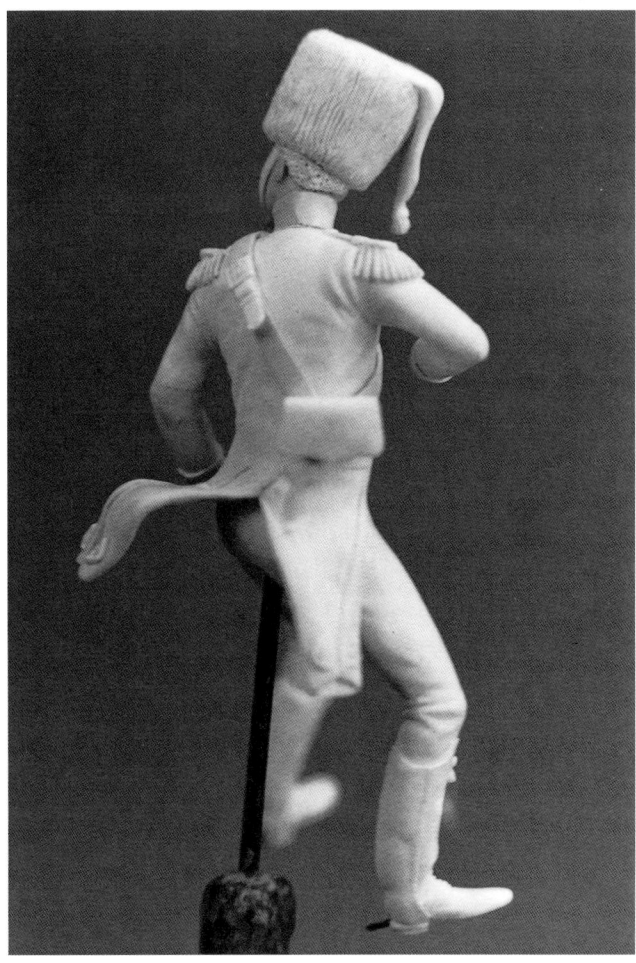

(Above) The headgear and cartridge box belting are added next. Note also the careful undercutting beneath the edges of the coat lapels and vest, to add relief. The sword belt buckle and plastic strip belting have been added around the waist.

(Above) The cartridge box and belt buckle attached, the lifted tongue of the belt giving added realism; and note the turn backs sculpted onto the new coattail.

(Below) If wished, before assembly the ears may be built up using very thin strings of putty to correct the rather flat-moulded appearance. The apparent but illusory mismatch between the sizes of the head and the headgear can be corrected simply by building up the hair at the back and creating sideburns.

currently producing 16 pairs of new resin hands in a variety of positions. These are available in the USA from The Red Lancers (see Note on Suppliers) or direct from Historex.

Historex **heads and headgear** are both nicely moulded and create no problems in themselves; however, when the two are combined it is obvious that something is amiss. The problem is the amount of hair moulded onto the figures' heads. When the headgear is added, the head looks too small or the headgear looks too large; neither is the case. Hair simply needs to be added, and this can be accomplished either with A+B putty or liquid sprue. I prefer the putty since it is

CHAPTER TWO: ASSEMBLY, DETAILING & ENHANCEMENT

(Above left) The chin scales are fitted tightly against the face and "fastened" with lead wire ties added beneath the chin. The epaulette fringes have been built up with A+B putty.

(Above) The hands have been fitted into the sleeve sockets after painting them separately; care was needed to align the sabre and scabbard from all angles - the slightest misalignment would immediately destroy the impression that the blade is full length inside the scabbard.

easier to work controllably. It's not possible or necessary to represent individual strands of hair, although I like to sculpt some relief into the putty. Sideburns and additional locks of hair can also be added.

Some modellers also prefer to enhance the rather flat-moulded ears (though personally I find that after headgear and corrected hair are applied this is seldom necessary). The rims can be built up carefully with tiny "strings" of putty. Alternatively, some modellers prefer to make a clean sweep; they carve the shape of a new ear into the end of a sprue, and then shave off very thin sections at a slight angle with a very sharp blade, setting them onto the head with liquid cement. Final trimming and shaping should be left until the new ears are quite dry and secure, whichever method is used.

If **chinscales** are indicated on the headgear, make certain you have the correct parts. There are any number of varying widths and designs, depending upon the headgear itself. Most are too thick and need to be reduced by sanding the inner surfaces. I like to use the kit scales if they are to hang untied from the headgear. If they are to be tied beneath the chin or tied onto the headgear itself I sometimes prefer to sculpt new ones. Don't forget the tied laces which secure them beneath the chin. Historex also supply excellent chains for lancer caps.

Historex provide a variety of separately moulded **cuffs** for jackets and coats, most of which are moulded in two parts. I have found it easier to sculpt new ones rather than glue these parts together, fill the join, and file the resulting cuffs into final shape. Gauntlets are moulded in a single piece, allowing them to be slipped over the hands.

After discarding the white tape provided in the kits for **belting and straps**, the obvious question is a replacement material. The choice depends upon several factors, including

CHAPTER TWO: ASSEMBLY, DETAILING & ENHANCEMENT

 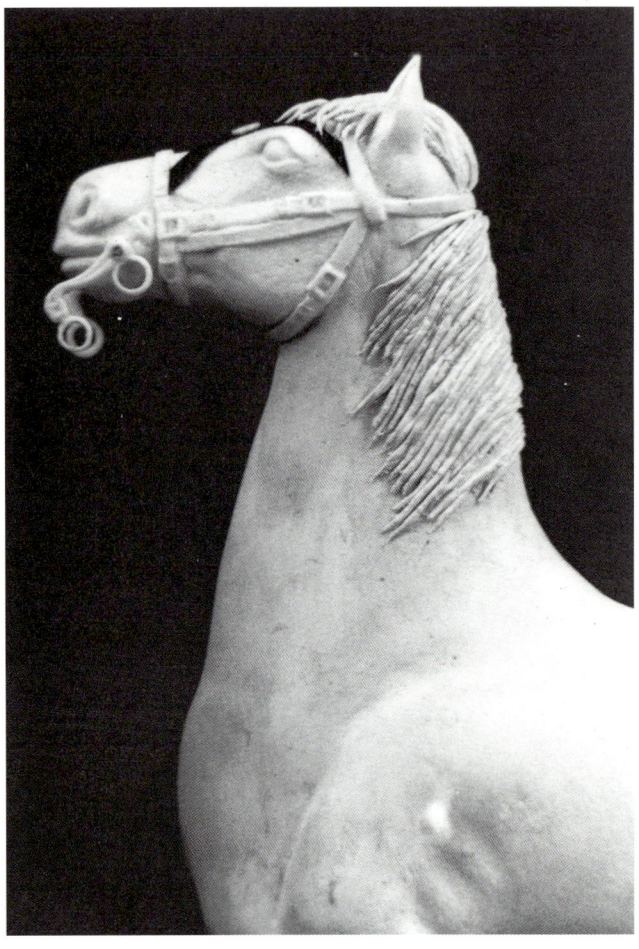

(Above left) Note the very small attachment point of the plume to the colpak; a small inserted section of insect pin strengthens this inevitably weak joint, and the plume was added as the very last part to avoid breakage. Notice the convincing impression of squinting into the distance created by the configuration of the eyes.

(Above) The Chasseur trumpeter's horse's head has been raised by repositioning the head atop the neck and raising the entire neck, filling the gaps with putty. Note the mane, which has been rebuilt using A+B putty, and the new harnessing across the face, added with paper.

personal taste, strength, familiarity with the material, location and possible attachments. I have used very thin plasticard, paper, and A+B putty, selecting whatever worked best for the task at hand. Whatever medium is selected, cut the belting into a slightly curved strip; this will provide a better fit and avoid gaps or wrinkling. It is often simpler to use two pieces instead of attempting a single belt, hiding the break beneath the buckle or epaulette. A+B putty can be rolled out in a thin sheet, allowed to become almost dry and then be sliced into appropriate widths. The semi-dry belt or strap is then applied around the body and super-glued into place. The choice of materials is up to the modeller.

Boots and shoes can add a lot of character and detail. The soles must first be filed flat and the heels cleaned up. As an added touch, roll out A+B putty and create a boot sole by applying a thin layer of putty to the bottom of the footwear in the approximate shape of the sole. Leave it to dry, and it can then be filed and sanded into the final shape. (It is also easy to create a realistically flopping or torn boot sole in this manner.) When completed, check the heels which may need to be built up slightly.

Cords and braiding present a problem; it is tricky to make them drape or hang with a realistic appearance of weight. The plastic representations supplied in the kits should be discarded in favour of some other material which is malleable and in scale. If the cording lies flat against the body and no part of it is suspended it can be sculpted from putty. If it is suspended I prefer to use either lead wire (well primed to prevent lead disease); strings of Duro's yellow/blue ribbon epoxy putty; or annealed brass wire (annealing simply involves heating the wire so that it bends more easily). Simulating cords is a matter of taste in this scale. If the wire is thin and strong enough it can actually be braided just like the real bullion cords. If not, a heavier strand can be painted to simulate the braiding. Attachment points are stronger if a single strand is inserted into a small hole drilled into the body or arm, ensuring the correct placement and lessening the need for glue.

Historex provide a variety of **epaulette straps and fringes**. Plain epaulettes without fringes - *contre-epaulettes* - should first be reduced in thickness. If the shoulder is raised and the epaulette represents soft cloth, it's easier to make a new one from A+B putty since the actual article would wrinkle and distort with the movement of the shoulder. If a fringe is indicated, cut away the moulded plastic fringe beneath the epaulette and discard it before gluing the epaulette to the shoulder. After attaching the epaulette, add a small amount of putty beneath the outside edge and press it into place. Wait until it is 50% cured, and then cut the vertical fringes into the putty. Cut the strands to the correct length and shape them to conform to the shoulder, spreading out the fringe if the pose dictates it.

Buttons are plentiful on Napoleonic uniforms, and any conversion or change in the uniform usually requires new buttons. If an entire row is needed, my favourite technique is to make them from putty. I first drill tiny holes with the tip of a new blade to mark the correct location and to give them a firm seat. Press a small dot of putty into each hole and mash it into a round button. Add the final shape with the tip of a wet brush. I have also used small bits of stretched plastic sprue, carefully cutting off slivers to represent buttons. The problem with this method is achieving consistent size, since a heated and stretched sprue has a tapered section, but it's an easy way to make one or two buttons quickly.

Finally, long, thin parts such as **weapons** can easily get bent in shipment or storage; but this can be corrected and, in fact, improved. For example, if a lance is required, remove the blade from the plastic shaft and replace the shaft with a length of steel wire. Drill out the base of the lance blade and super-glue it to the new wire shaft. Muskets can also be improved by adding bulk to the stock. Remember to drill out the muzzles of all firearms with the tip of a No.11 blade.

MOUNTED FIGURES

Most of the assembly tips apply to mounted figures. One of the more important areas concerns the **height of the rider**. Historex produces interchangeable bodies for foot and mounted figures. As a result, the mounted figures always looked a little too "tall in the saddle". In real life a sitting figure appears to compress somewhat due to the weight bearing directly on the spine, and the easiest way to simulate this adjustment is by removing between 1/16in and 3/32in from the top of the assembled legs. After gluing the leg halves together, use a razor saw to remove the excess; you may have to make a slight adjustment to

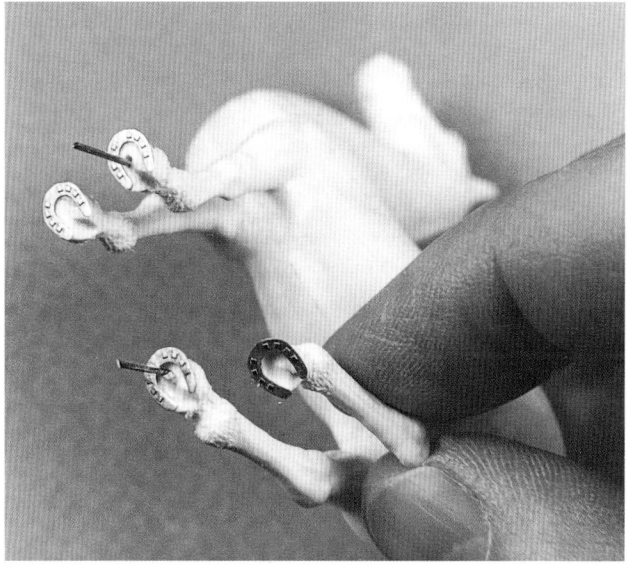

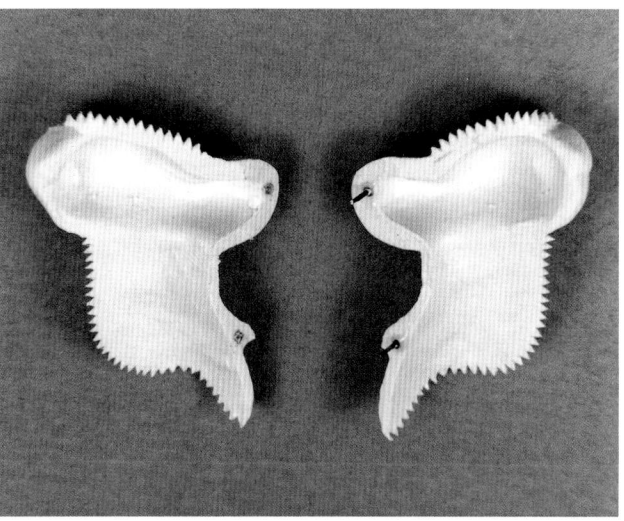

(Above left) Historex now offer etched brass horseshoes, which are best attached using epoxy cement. Note the two hooves drilled and pinned, to strengthen the final attachment to the base.

(Left) Increasing the horse's girth means that the saddle has to be correspondingly widened. Pins have been positioned to help in final alignment of the two halves.

CHAPTER TWO: ASSEMBLY, DETAILING & ENHANCEMENT

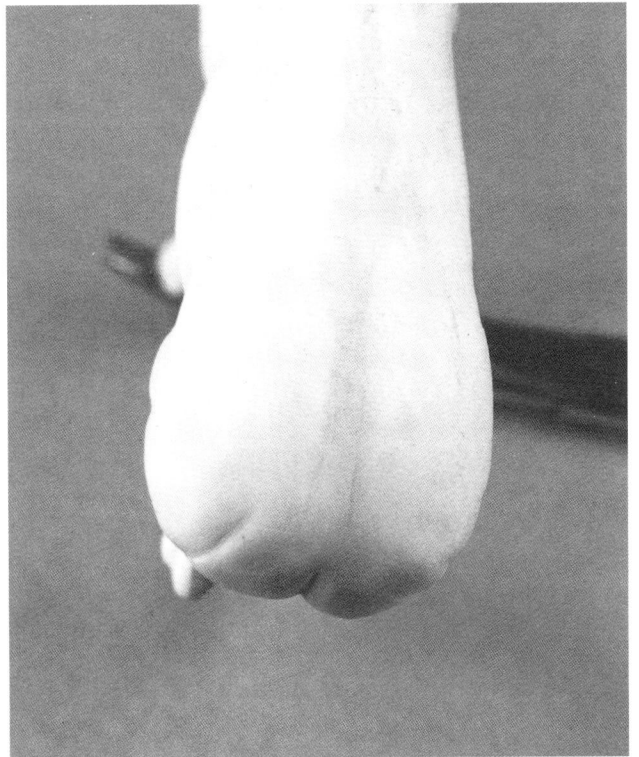

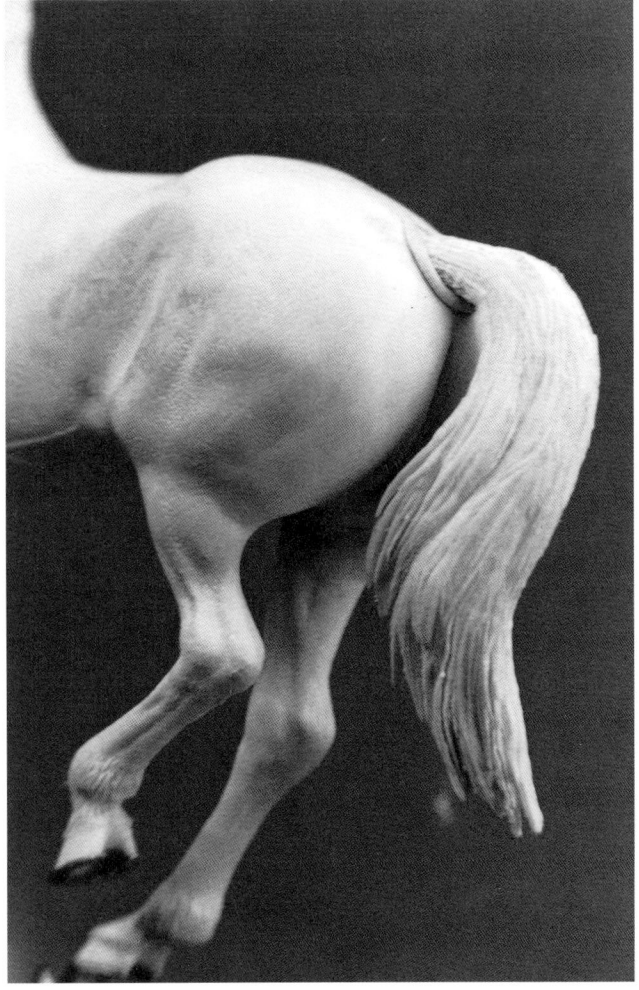

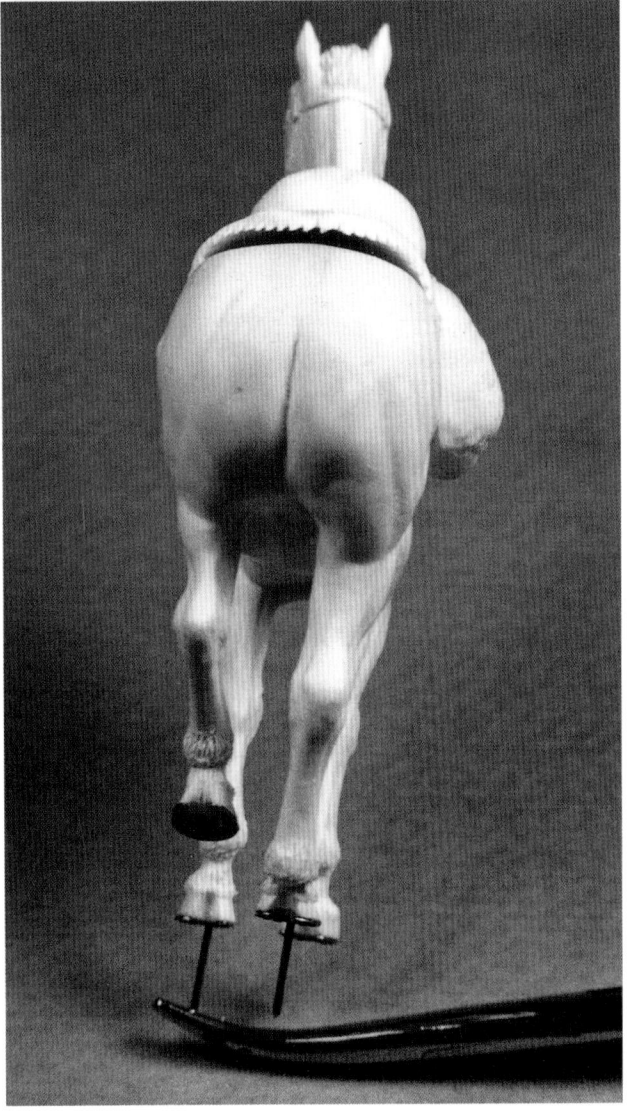

(Top left and left) The entire width of the horse body has been increased by adding a plastic shim between the horse halves and filling with A+B putty. The modification of the horse's back and the saddle inevitably result in a noticeable gap between them.

(Above) The gap is filled by building up the horse's rump with A+B putty. The crupper has been added beneath the tail, which is enhanced with additional pyrogravuring.

the remaining portion of the leg tops when attaching the torso, but this is a minor chore. The result is a more natural rider who appears relaxed and in scale with the horse.

Before adding the head and arms, a critical step is to check the **rider's seat** - his position in the saddle: does he sit in the saddle, or is he perched delicately atop it as if trying to avoid sitting on a hot stove? Remember that the model represents a heavy object with a malleable surface pressing down against a relatively more rigid surface; at the point of contact he should almost appear part of the saddle itself. One way to accomplish this is to add bulk to the rider's buttocks. As moulded they are somewhat on the sparse side, and the addi-

CHAPTER TWO: ASSEMBLY, DETAILING & ENHANCEMENT

(Left) The completed saddle. Note the sharpening of the fancy "wolf's-teeth" fabric fringe to the sheepskin saddle cover; the "fluffy" effect of the fleece after careful work with the hot needle tip of the pyrogravure; and the reattachment of the backrest after modification.

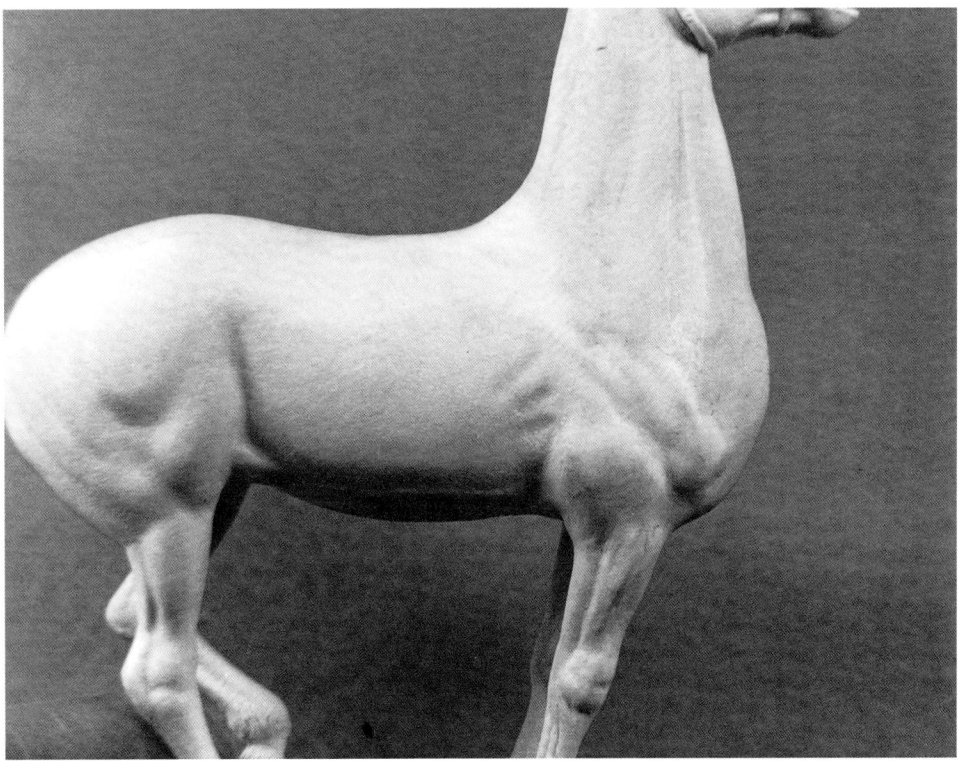

(Right) The right front leg was repositioned to alter the horse's stance, and the muscles rebuilt. The elegant lines of the Historex horse are evident here.

tion of A+B putty not only corrects the deficiency but also helps to fill any remaining air space between rider and saddle. When the rider is totally assembled, any remaining gaps can be filled by using Five Minute epoxy cement when gluing the rider to the saddle. The slower curing epoxy also has the advantage of allowing the rider to be moved into the correct position before the glue sets.

Next, attach the body to the completed legs. In deciding upon the final pose, remember that you have several choices when building a standard Historex figure. The **selection of torso** can give variety of appearance without your committing yourself to a major conversion. Depending upon this choice, your rider can be leaning or turning in the saddle - not every torso has to be facing front, and even the regular bodies can be turned slightly without additional conversion surgery becoming necessary. Look carefully at the choices of available bodies in the Historex Spare Parts Illustrated Catalogue before making your selection. The legs should be glued to the body using liquid plastic cement. This may seem a minor point, but you need a strong weld if you want to guard against breaking the join while working on the figure at later stages. Let these parts dry overnight before going to the next step.

The figure's **coattails and turnbacks** should

CHAPTER TWO: ASSEMBLY, DETAILING & ENHANCEMENT

(Right) With the addition of the bit, the completed horse ready for painting.

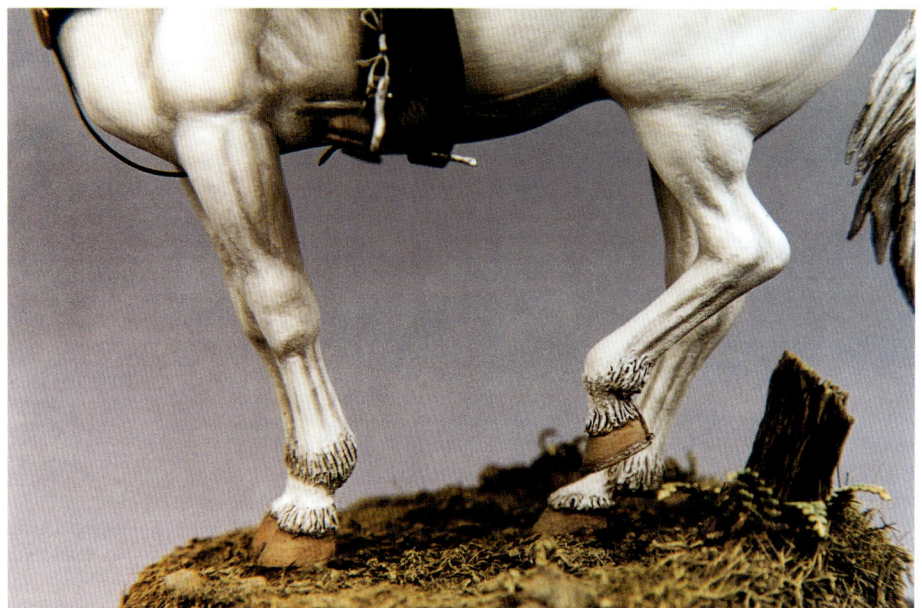

(Left) The fetlocks were additionally detailed with the pyrogravure for easier highlighting during painting.

(Right) Note the boot soles added with A+B putty; and the details of the stirrup leather, all added with small strips of paper. The white-painted straps and slings repay subtle shading to bring out their contours convincingly.

CHAPTER TWO: ASSEMBLY, DETAILING & ENHANCEMENT

slight adjustment or correction to complete the pose.

For example, look at the arm in relation to the reins. Is the hand a natural extension of the arm? No matter what position is selected, follow the same rule for the hands discussed in the previous section - remove them from the arms and rework them until they are convincing and natural.

The same approach also applies when attaching the **head** to the body. Depending upon the pose, slight variations can occur in the head's tilt, adding additional character and attitude

(Left) Before the rider was attached all the harnessing and reins were made from paper with Historex buckles added, painted, and then attached.

(Below) The completed "Trumpeter, 20th Chasseurs à Cheval". This model is in fact a tribute to an actual soldier, who was renowned for his swordplay and his fine grey charger. The horse survived the 1812 Russian campaign - his rider did not.

be attached next. This is a little more difficult, especially in the case of mounted figures. The positioning, attachment and draping of coattails requires some extra forethought. First, the two parts usually do not fit snugly or drape naturally as supplied in the kit. Additional filling and correction with A+B putty is required after attaching them to the body with super-glue. After test-fitting both coattails over and around the saddle and valise, fair them smoothly onto the torso. This may require several trial fittings; it is important to be certain that the tails fit naturally in relation to the body, saddle and valise, or the figure may end up with flying coattails on a standing horse, or drooping coattails on a galloping horse. The same rules apply for both standing and running foot figures as well.

If new coattails need to be made due to radical modifications, roll out A+B putty and let it almost cure. Cut it into the shape of a new coattail and super-glue it to the body before it completely cures, draping it into final position. If turnbacks are needed add them with more putty once the new part has cured.

Fitting the **arms** is a crucial step. The figure's fluidity in both active and relaxed attitudes is a combination of many factors, but the arms tell much of the story. This is not a simple question of gluing the arms to the body. More radical conversions are discussed in the next chapter, but stock figures may also need

CHAPTER TWO: ASSEMBLY, DETAILING & ENHANCEMENT

Detail from the author's model "The Sharp End" (see Chapter Five), showing the impression of independent movement of suspended items - such as the cartridge box and the sabre on its slings - which Historex's separate parts allow during construction of the figure.

to the pose. Attaching the head to the body with a pin creates the correct position, and also provides a rigid armature when correcting or resculpting the collar. Remember that in real life the collar's opening remains largely at the front, the head turning within the collar. If you choose to turn the head this will mean cutting a new opening into the existing Historex collar, which is moulded onto the head part, or resculpting the entire collar.

Small parts such as **swords, stirrups, carbines**, etc., can also be enhanced. For example, in addition to thinning the sword blade the handguard can be improved by careful trimming or filing of the bars, which vastly improves the delicacy and scale appearance of the weapon.

Adding the sword, sabretache or carbine should be one of the last steps after the figure is painted (see the suggested assembly sequence at the end of this chapter). Add these items after the figure is glued to the saddle; this may take careful handling, but you avoid a lot of awkward painting if you wait until this stage. Adding them to the model so that they hang naturally is one of the secrets to producing a better mounted figure. Take a few extra moments to be certain that all positioning of attached gear is correct, as dictated by weight and gravity.

Attaching sword and sabretache slings is a critical procedure that takes a little practice. First, open the rings on the sabretache and sword scabbard; instead of using a small rattail file I prefer to use the tip of a new No.11 blade, delicately swivelling it around each side of the ring to gently enlarge the opening. Yes, you will occasionally break the ring, but it can be glued back together; or you may prefer to make a replacement wire ring. Loop small gauge brass or copper wire several times around a small dowel or toothpick. Slide the looped wire off and cut away several "rings" using a No.11 blade. Gently close the loop and, voila, you have a strong brass ring.

The best material to create reins, slings and straps is a good grade of typing paper. Much of the realism depends upon recreating leather in the proper scale and connecting it to the bit, scabbard, sabretache or other attachment points. Cut strips of paper into 6in lengths using a metal ruler and new No.11 blade. Painting them using acrylics will also serve to strengthen the paper - in fact, a painted strap or rein will actually break a plastic ring before the paper tears. Measure the correct length; then connect it by making a small loop through the ring, gluing the paper to itself with a water-soluble "white glue". Leave the loop open around the ring so that the paper swivels freely until you're ready for the final positioning. For parts such as the scabbard and sabretache I find it easier to add the straps to the rings and then attach the entire assembly to the figure. You may then need to add a dot of super-glue inside the ring, pulling the rein or strap tight to be certain that it has the correct drape.

Attaching paper straps to a model figure is a delicate process. For example, attaching sabretache slings against the body can be frustrating. First remove a small amount of paint from the attachment area, then add a small dot of

CHAPTER TWO: ASSEMBLY, DETAILING & ENHANCEMENT

Max Longhurst, Great Britain:

"I started to make Historex figures about 25 years ago. I had made my yearly pilgrimage to the Model Engineer Exhibition to buy material for my model railway; and on the way out I noticed a stand selling little figures. I went over for a closer look at the finished figures, made by the French modeller Pierre Conrad. I immediately bought a kit; I was so enthusiastic that I built and painted it as soon as I got home. I took it back the next day to compare it to Conrad's figures - and realized that I had a long, long way to go. I introduced myself to Lynn Sangster on the stand; he gave me lots of help and advice, and I have been making Historex figures ever since.

"I love to build scenes from paintings of the Napoleonic period, which involves a lot of conversion work. The main tool I use is the pyrogravure, for bending limbs, adding plastic, and taking it away. For fur and hair effects my pyrogravure is filed to a fine point. To achieve these I first 'paint' liquid plastic - made by mixing a solvent and scrap plastic in a small bottle - onto the surface, and then style it with the pyrogravure.

"I paint using oils throughout. I do not use silver or gold metallics, preferring to use yellows and browns for gold effects, and black, white and Prussian Blue for silver or metal effects. I do not use any medium but apply the oils straight from the tube. I also undercoat in oils in the final colour I will be applying; I find this gives a strong colour. As a result, I am always waiting for things to dry.

"A small tip for beginners: Historex kits come with insignia sprues, and it is worth studying the smaller parts, as they come in handy for many other things. Some parts, like buckles for instance, are better than others, and sprues can be purchased separately. And if there's one final rule, it's don't be afraid to experiment."

Max Longhurst's "Horse Grenadier of the Guard".

super-glue, pressing the tip of the sling onto the figure using a toothpick. You may also have to touch up the area with paint afterwards.

Additional enhancement

A+B epoxy putty has innumerable uses in working with Historex figures. The best variety is produced by Gemline, and can be found in hardware stores and appliance repair shops. It comes in several colours including white, which I like best when working with the white Historex plastic. I get a better sense of how the figure is progressing; and it has a finer grain, fairing easily onto plastic surfaces. However, other putty colours work just as well; and British modellers achieve excellent results

This very cold "Brunswick Hussar" remains one of the author's favourite pieces. The horse was modified to gather its legs beneath the body to emphasize the cold weather; tail, forelock, throat tassel and shako plume all "blow" in the same direction, creating the impression of a harsh wind. A small cape was fashioned from A+B putty around the hussar's shoulders. Note the icicle, made from Five Minute epoxy, hanging from the branch.

CHAPTER TWO: ASSEMBLY, DETAILING & ENHANCEMENT

with the local equivalent, Milliput.

Working with this type of putty is relatively easy once you get used to it. Be certain always to mix equal parts of the two elements thoroughly, and to wash the residue off your fingers before handling the figure. I apply and smooth out larger surfaces by simply wetting my finger and pressing the putty onto the surface. Smaller areas can be faired into place using a wet paintbrush (an old one). Folds and creases are added with homemade tools such as shaped toothpicks or an insect pin pushed into a small dowel, and further contoured using a small wet paintbrush. I allow all puttied surfaces to cure for 24 hours before carving or sanding them. Frankly, I long ago gave up trying to accelerate drying with applied heat. Historex plastic has a low melting point, and even a little distortion will ruin hours of work. It is better to be patient, and you can always work on another part of the model while the putty cures.

Another way to enhance the figure is to look for areas where undercutting will emphasize relief. Undercutting is a simple technique which improves the three-dimensional appearance of moulded-on detail. Pockets, flaps or division lines are enhanced by using the back of the knife blade to scrape beneath the edge of the raised detail to make it more prominent. Painting the area then becomes much easier and improves the definition.

HORSES

Historex's strongest appeal to many painters is their line of cavalry figures. The ability to recreate Napoleonic cavalrymen provides a strong lure to those with a fascination for horse and rider; and the key word here is "horse". Recreating a realistic cavalryman depends heavily on an accurate representation of the horse; since the mount is roughly four times larger than the rider, it stands to reason that a poorly modelled or painted horse will overwhelm the appearance of a meticulously painted rider.

Historex produce a wide variety of horses. They are moulded in superb detail and include enough musculature to keep the pickiest painter happy. Little cleaning up is needed other than run-of-the-mill mouldline removal and filing. If there is a bone to pick regarding their accuracy it centres on their general size. While they are in scale, they tend to be slightly delicate, representing Arabian thoroughbreds rather than everyday horses. For senior officers the thoroughbred may be appropriate, but for other ranks the horseflesh was of distinctly less delicate quality. This overall deficiency in size and robust appearance is magnified if heavy cavalry is depicted. There is a definite need for a heavier horse. Converting stock Historex horses into heavier animals will be covered in the next chapter, however; here we deal with basic assembly techniques. The stock horse provided in the kit will paint up quite nicely in most instances.

Begin by scraping and filing off the mould-lines. Notch a "V" into the rear of all **hooves**, and drill a slight indentation into the bottom of any hooves which are visible when lifted off the ground. Horseshoes are provided, including new brass ones; the old plastic shoes need to be cleaned up and carefully fitted, and I prefer the new brass type. Attach them using Five Minute epoxy to ensure the best adhesion. Next, use the pyrogravure to texture hair onto the **fetlocks** and over the front of the hooves. Do this before you assemble the halves in order to avoid accidentally damaging the legs.

Assemble the two **body halves**, using liquid plastic cement for the strongest bond. Build up the belly slightly, using A+B putty to add a little more weight to the horse. All other seams can then be filled with putty and sanded smooth. One additional Historex part that seems to puzzle many modellers is the horse genitalia. Not all horses are mares; if you're

---

(Opposite top) A most influential diorama: the amazing "Eve of Essling" by Shep Paine, which featured more than 30 mounted Historex figures including many individual senior officers and personalities known to have been at that battle in 1809. The clever lighting of this photograph simulates the thin sunlight of a cold spring day in northern Europe, and brings out the excellent groundwork.

(Bottom left) One of the personalities in Paine's "Eve of Essling": Col. LeJeune illustrates the amount of lace and facial detail possible with careful painting.

(Bottom right) Two staff officers on the "Eve of Essling". Note the entirely convincing impression of a conversation taking place, created simply by careful observation of the angles of heads and bodies. There is no extreme animation; this sort of effect is within the reach of any modeller who really uses his eyes - it's just that until Shep Paine demonstrated it, few modellers had grasped what could be achieved with Historex.

CHAPTER TWO: ASSEMBLY, DETAILING & ENHANCEMENT

CHAPTER TWO: ASSEMBLY, DETAILING & ENHANCEMENT

A beautiful "French Kettledrummer" by Bill Liebold.

building a stallion, check the parts sprues carefully - the required male part is provided.

The **head** should be selected next. There is a wide choice, but some do not look quite right with certain bodies; spend a few minutes making certain you have a believable pose. Carefully scrape off the mouldlines on the head. Some of the straps can be slightly reduced by filing them down, but be careful not to lose the subtle detail and moulded-on buckles. If the mouth is closed it doesn't need any attention beyond basic cleaning up. If the mouth is open there are several ways to improve the appearance.

As supplied in the kit, the **mouth** is filled with plastic residue from the moulding process. This should be removed with a knife and drill. Teeth can be added using A+B putty, but remember that only the upper and lower *front* teeth can be seen. If you want to open the mouth of a closed-mouth head, remove the lower jaw and reattach it in an open mode with the help of a little A+B putty. (As with all these steps, it goes without saying that you should keep good pictorial sources handy for frequent reference during this process.)

If a closed-mouth head is selected, use a root canal bit to drill a hole into the head at the back of the mouth. Insert a short length of a shirt pin so that about 1/16in of the pin protrudes on each side (if the mouth is open, simply glue a length of pin into the rear of the mouth). Before attaching the bits reduce their inside thickness, and drill a small hole in the boss of each one with the tip of a No.11 blade. Glue the bits to the pin with super-glue; then rebuild the boss with a flattened ball of putty. Check the angle of the bridle bit in relation to the horse's mouth; it should almost parallel the mouth, not hanging down at a sharp angle unless the reins are completely relaxed or hanging loose to the ground.

Several types of **ears** are provided, which are placed into notches in the horses' heads. The ears are nicely moulded and care should be taken to keep them sharp and intact when cleaning them up. The fit is good, but there is always a small gap that needs to be filled with putty.

The **mane and forelock** supplied in the kit can be used, but I prefer to create new ones using A+B putty. To convert the mane, roll out a length of putty and press it into position on one side of the neck - don't worry about the fit or appearance at this stage. Flatten it with a moist fingertip until it is approximately 1/16in thick. Allow the putty to cure for about 30 minutes before beginning to texture it with a sharp No.11 blade. Be careful not to make the hair too uniform. Trim the length along the neck and fair the mane onto the ridge along the neck. When cured, you can add additional thin strings of putty to overlap the bridle strap or build up the area. The forelock over the brow is added in the same manner, lifting it slightly when almost cured for added depth.

Historex horse **tails** can be modified or heated for different configurations and texture added with a pyrogravure. Insert a short length of pin into the horse's rump for extra strength, drilling a matching hole into the tail; attach it with super-glue and add putty to the tail's base, smoothing it onto the rump.

The **crupper** is the rolled leather brace from the rear of the saddle which fits beneath the horse's tail to help align the saddle. The simplest way to make this is to roll out a thin length of A+B putty, creating a string about an inch longer than needed for easier handling. Let it cure for about 30-40 minutes. Loop it under the tail, bringing it together over the horse's rump. Press the parallel lengths together and cut them off about 1/4in past the tail. Super-glue the crupper beneath the tail

CHAPTER TWO: ASSEMBLY, DETAILING & ENHANCEMENT

(Right and below) Paper slings and reins have the advantage of being flexible and strong when painted with acrylics, and easily assume the correct "drape" to represent the weight of a sword or the tension in the rider's grip on the reins.

(Right) The shabraque - ornamental saddle cloth - has been reduced in thickness by working from the inside surface of the plastic, to obtain the correct scale impression of fabric at the visible edges.

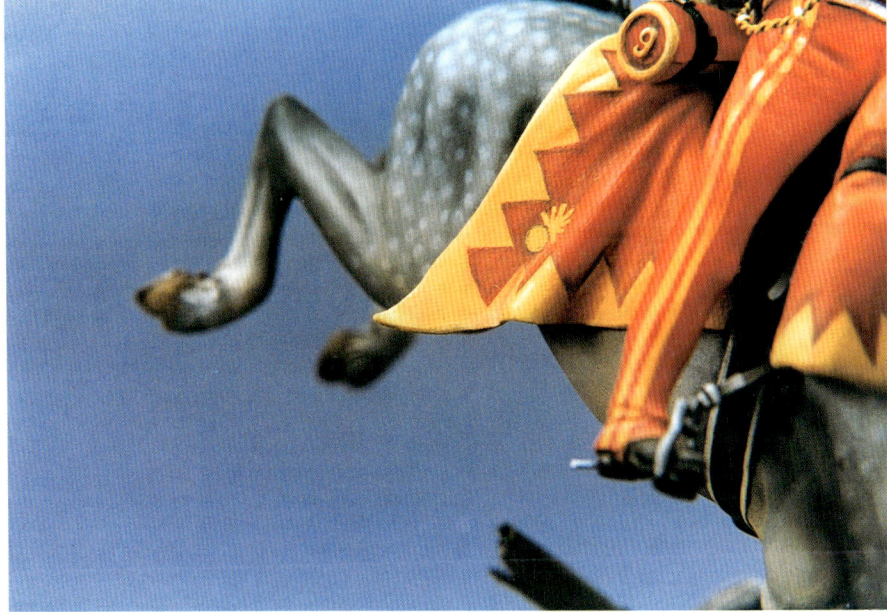

CHAPTER TWO: ASSEMBLY, DETAILING & ENHANCEMENT

(Top left) Additional ornamentation for officers' horse furniture - which was often very rich, reflecting the individual's wealth - can be created with metallic paint carefully applied in a somewhat stiffer consistency.

(Above) Another illustration of a shabraque, the end of which has been heated and bent to create a sense of movement in the cloth.

(Left) The final appearance of details such as the firmly grasping hand, the flying trumpet cords and pelisse, and the pyrogravured fur is worth the additional time taken over them.

CHAPTER TWO: ASSEMBLY, DETAILING & ENHANCEMENT

when dry. The remaining portion of the crupper is later added with paper or putty so that the strap disappears beneath the saddle. Add buckles or other details as indicated to hide the joint.

The other various saddle, **harness** and miscellaneous straps are made from paper as described previously. Reins, breast band straps, girth, stirrup leathers, hitching rein, ornamental straps, etc. may be glued into place either before or after the saddle is added, depending upon how much they interfere with painting. Personally, I add them after the horse and saddle are painted and glued into position.

If the rider's left hand is holding the reins, first glue the figure into place before attaching the reins to the hand. Think of the action being portrayed, since that will affect the drape: are they stretched tightly or hanging loose? The final positioning will be affected by the pose. I find it easier to fix the final position by super-gluing the reins to the ring itself, thus ensuring the placement. In a standing pose where one set of the reins is draped over the front of the saddle, gluing this set to the saddle ensures their correct placement (in the French system the shorter bridoon rein was used only to pull up the horse's head).

I prefer to use the buckles provided by Historex after first reducing their thickness. Paint the buckle area in metallic tones, glue them to the appropriate strap or rein, and finally paint the leather colour in the center. Other modellers prefer making their own buckles from putty - it's a purely personal choice.

Several types of **stirrups** are provided according to the subject. After removing the mould lines, reduce the thickness of the bottom of the stirrup with a file. If you want to be super-accurate you can drill out the bottom of each to form a stirrup ring; it depends on how far you want to carry the detailing on a part that won't be seen except in extreme action poses (at some point you have to ask yourself, where does this madness end?. . .) The stirrup leathers are made from paper, and a surprisingly large amount of detail can be added to represent the adjusting straps and buckles; not all stirrups or leathers are the same, so review your references carefully. You can attach the upper ends of the stirrup leathers to the rider so that the tops disappear along the insides of the legs. If you want still more accuracy you can run the straps beneath the saddle, modifying the shabraque or saddlecloth accordingly.

Saddles

I prefer to build the saddle separately, not attaching it to the horse until both are painted. It's easier to paint the saddle and horse in this manner, especially if the saddle includes small detail or lines of lace. I also like to paint the horse unencumbered by the saddle. There are, however, exceptions to any rule. If the saddle is heavily modified or tightly fitted next to the horse's body, it is easier to build the saddle directly onto the horse.

Historex moulds saddles in both one- and two-piece units. The two-piece saddles allow more leeway in conversions since they can adjusted more easily. If radical plastic surgery requires modification of a one-piece saddle, it is simpler to cut it in half front to rear, repositioning the halves into a new unit (see next chapter).

As mentioned earlier, mould lines and flash on the shabraque or saddlecloth should be scraped off and sanded smooth. The overall appearance is further improved by reducing the thickness of the cloth to bring it into scale. File and sand the inner surfaces which hang down; it's not necessary to reduce the entire unit. Animation of the cloth is accomplished by carefully holding the lower 1/4in or 1/2in against a 100 watt light bulb for 15-20 seconds, quickly bending the end around a curved surface (dowel, knife handle, etc.) to curl the edge. Avoid sharp angles - they are not realistic.

Valises and blanket rolls require careful fitting. Again, be certain that these items do not suffer from apparent weightlessness: add a little A+B putty beneath these items to increase the underside area. Let it cure for 30-40 minutes, wet both surfaces, and then gently press the item temporarily into position to get a tight fit. Remove the piece, let it cure completely, and then file it to final shape, rechecking the fit until you are satisfied.

If the saddle is covered with a sheepskin then use the pyrogravure to texture the surface. It may be necessary to add liquid sprue over modified areas before pyrogravuring. It's a somewhat arduous process, but the final effect warrants the work. Once the rider and saddle are painted and permanently in place, go back with the pyrogravure around the edges of the rider (with *great* care not to ruin your work. .), pulling up additional strands of the sheepskin around his legs and buttocks; this will give the appearance that the rider is firmly seated. Touch up with paint where necessary.

If fur saddle holsters are present, pyrogravure each separately before attaching them; drill a hole into each, and corresponding holes into the saddle to align the attachments. Fix each holster to the saddle with a short length of pin. Check your references to be certain how the holsters were attached to the saddle, since there was usually a connecting strap over the pommel.

When the saddle is complete, be certain that it fits tightly to the horse. This always raises the question: is it easier to make an adjustment to the horse or to the saddle? Since the saddle blanket, shabraque or saddlecloth has to remain within a certain tolerance at the edges, it's simpler to modify the horse's rump (croup and loins) for necessary adjustments. Fit the saddle to the horse and check for space beneath it. Mark the areas to be built up with a pencil, remove the saddle, and build up the indicated area with A+B putty faired onto the horse. Generously wet both the saddle and putty (I use saliva - disgusting, but more effective than water) and press the saddle firmly back into place. Check the fit again; remove the saddle once again and rework the putty until the fit is tight. Let the putty cure and sand it smooth.

When this area is completed, check the fit where the front of the saddle meets the horse's neck - there is usually a gap here which needs filling. However, in this instance it's easier to build up the underside of the saddle as opposed to reworking the horse's neck. Getting a tight fit in both areas is crucial to the final appearance.

Be extra careful when attaching the saddle to the horse. It is all too easy to align the saddle improperly, which in turn produces an off-centre rider. Using Five Minute epoxy allows the additional time to position the saddle correctly and provides a firm bond.

When you are ready to attach the horse to the base, drill holes into one or two legs and insert short lengths of pin. When corresponding holes are drilled in the groundwork, make them oversize and fill with Five Minute epoxy; this allows additional time and leeway for exact positioning.

The final step before painting is to wash off the accumulated sanding dust and grit; there can be a surprising amount of this on a completed figure. Hold the assembled parts beneath fast-running warm water, shake off the excess water, and let the parts dry overnight before painting.

Greg DiFranco, USA:

"To me Historex represents more than miniature figure kits. It is an entire medium of the hobby, just as oil paint is to fine art...It is such a unique form of modelling, and so flexible. It offers the modeller the opportunity to create a one-of-a-kind, originally conceived model, all without having to create the intricate details and components of a figure from scratch. The contribution this line of figures has made to the artistic advancement of the hobby is great.

"Major Jolly" by Greg DiFranco. (Photo Phil Kessling)

So many of the most influential artists in the hobby have honed their skills on conversions, scratch-building, vignettes and dioramas using Historex kits - this modeller certainly did.

"When I began in the hobby in the 1960s, I can remember reading how difficult it was to make a Historex model, how there were so many small parts and no assembly instructions. Let's face it: Historex was not for the novice or beginner then, and to this day still is not. But after seeing a number of these beautiful white models assembled but unpainted in the Polk's hobby shop display case in New York I decided I had to have a try. The first model, a mounted Marshal Saint Cyr (which I still have), was difficult to make but so different and intriguing. The detail was awe-inspiring. It wasn't until I saw Shep Paine's 'Eve of Essling' diorama that I realized what a powerful medium Historex was; the numerous figures - all in different poses, many mounted - were an amazing sight for a teenage modeller.

"Since then, I have created (note the word created) many models from these kits and used their parts innumerable times. Every Historex I have created is special to me because each has my own stamp of originality on it, whether I simply cut and bend an arm, or go all the way and resculpt major portions of the model.

"Of all the range the parts I like and use most are the horse components... The great thing about them, and the attribute that make them so timeless, is that the basic anatomy is very good. The musculature is excellent, and the ease of conversion is exceptional due to the numerous horse halves available. So many poses can be made by just mixing and matching the horse halves; and if one of these doesn't happen to work for you, the leg positions can be changed easily with a saw and putty. I personally like to choose from the hundreds of positions illustrated in the classic photo study book by Muybridge. I also like many of the horse heads; one or two are perfect for heavy horse heads, and others have the sloped noses associated with Arabians.

"Historex offers the modeller the pieces needed to create almost any figure that can be conjured up in their mind. All that is necessary is some creativity, modelling skills, and a lot of patience."

CHAPTER TWO: ASSEMBLY, DETAILING & ENHANCEMENT

(Above) The standard Historex pelisse has been modified so that the sleeves are blowing in the wind and jolting of his gallop, the sense of movement further reinforced by the suspension of the sabretache and the "flounders" on the headgear. When a heavily-accoutered rider covers the ground at speed everything on man and horse alike bounces and flaps.

(Left) The wind-ruffled appearance of this horse's mane was achieved using A+B putty.

CHAPTER TWO: ASSEMBLY, DETAILING & ENHANCEMENT

(Above) Painting an animal pelt requires additional research and some patience, as evidenced by this very ornate tigerskin shabraque forming part of Murat's horse furniture. Details such as the unusual twisted scabbard cords, made from soft lead wire, add distinctive realism.

(Right) Saddles are usually best constructed and painted separately, but this Prussian Landwehr saddle was built onto the horse due to the unusually large wolf's-teeth edging, parts of which are modelled for a suspended effect.

CHAPTER TWO: ASSEMBLY, DETAILING & ENHANCEMENT

Assembly sequence

A careful assembly sequence can make many tasks easier, especially if the subject is a mounted figure. You can avoid headaches and major errors if you follow some rules before you begin assembling the figure. There may be a better assembly sequence, but the following one works for me:

1) Build the horse first, adding everything except loose straps, slings and reins.
2) Build the saddle assembly, test fit it to the horse, and adjust as necessary.
3) Assemble the rider - legs, body, head and arms in that order.
   Make certain that the rider has a good seat in the saddle by test fitting before adding a lot of detail.
4) Add the remaining detail to the figure with the exception of suspended straps and slings - painting around them is extremely challenging.
5) Fit the valise on the saddle. Attach it temporarily so that the rider's coattails drape properly around it. Remove it for painting.
6) Test fit and add all other parts to the rider and horse unless they project awkwardly (e.g. lances), or are exposed to easy breakage (e.g. plumes) - put these aside for attachment later.
7) Paint the horse and set it aside to dry.
8) Paint small parts to be attached later.
9) Paint the saddle.
10) Paint the rider.
11) Attach the saddle to the horse after both have dried.
12) Attach the rider to the saddle.
13) Complete the groundwork and paint it.
14) Attach the figure to the base.
15) Add the reins, harnessing, sabretache, scabbard and other protruding parts.
16) Add final touches with pastels or oils, blending the groundwork up onto the lower legs.

CHAPTER THREE
CONVERTING

Many of the assembly tips previously discussed include suggestions which technically might be called "conversions". There is sometimes a thin line between enhancing and converting. Almost any figure may require some additional work. A lot of the modification work covered in the previous chapter can be attributed to my preference for improving the basic figure. This chapter, however, covers new poses or the creation of a totally different figure, this being the more standard definition of "conversions". Being a reconstructed plastic modeller, the opportunity to convert a stock figure is a lure that I cannot resist, especially given the size and versatility of the range of available parts and the ease of working the styrene material. Converting foot or mounted figures may involve any number of changes; this chapter describes conversion of a mounted subject, but the basic techniques apply to standing figures.

The inspiration for a conversion can come from many sources. The drive to create something unique can originate with an illustration, an account of a historical incident, a daydream or a brainstorm. Whatever the inspiration, successfully recreating an idea in three-dimensional form first requires a basic understanding of anatomy. The modeller must be certain that the pose "works"; you can have every limb in correct proportion, but the conversion will fail if the positioning is incorrect or improbable. It is critical that the anatomy be correct, and this may require assembling and disassembling the figure several times until you get it right. Time spent in this somewhat excruciating process is critical to the outcome. Inspect your work from all angles, and get a second opinion if you're uncertain.

I prefer using Historex parts whenever possible as opposed to sculpting entirely new parts, and the method discussed here will involve changing existing components of the range rather than making new ones.

Horses

For mounted figures, build the horse and saddle first. The reason is twofold. Firstly, I usually convert the horse extensively, increasing its girth, changing the neck, etc.; this necessitates converting the saddle, which in turn requires some conversion of the rider's legs. Secondly, the pose and attitude of the rider are controlled to a great degree by what the horse is doing. Converting a rider without considering the horse's actions can lead to a failed conversion.

Whimsically titled "Gunther, Max, and Great Aunt Freda", this piece was especially done for my wife, who is the proud owner of a dachshund! The Prussian Landwehr cavalryman is a Historex conversion, as is the woman; the dog is scratchbuilt.

CHAPTER THREE: CONVERTING

(Top left) A close-up of the modified shako and lengthened coat, achieved with A+B putty, and the dachshund sculpted in A+B over a wire armature. The hand holding the dog was carefully re-sculpted to give the appearance of a firm grasp.

(Above) Historex's Peasant Woman was converted extensively into a shorter woman, slightly stooped. The body was severed at the waist, bent forwards, and tilted to one side, and approximately 1/4in was removed from the legs. The facial details were also considerably altered.

As stated in Chapter Two, Historex horses are a little on the fragile side for military use. Increasing their size, however, is not that difficult. The standard method is to cement a plastic shim between the body halves, and I add a 1/16in to 3/32in plastic insert. In fact, the plastic base provided by Historex will provide a piece of about the right thickness unless you are building a much heavier animal. Don't be too concerned about appearance as you glue the spacer into place, just make certain the halves are aligned properly and let the assembly dry. When it is fully cured you can cut away any excess and fill the remaining seam with A+B putty. File and sand into final shape.

Next, consider the horse's head. Whether you're planning to use a standard kit head or a modified one, the neck will have to be correspondingly increased if the body is widened. This is essential where the neck joins the body. Since the neck's thickness is increased, the added putty will obscure the existing neck muscles. Fair the putty onto the neck from the horse's body, making a smooth transition. Consult your references on horses and study the neck muscles; resculpting them is not as difficult as it might first appear. Using a burnisher or any rounded instrument, gently press the muscle outlines into the wet putty, smoothing them out with a wet brush. Sand smooth after the putty cures.

If the horse's head is to be turned, cut the head away from the existing neck just behind the rear halter strap and drill a hole in the back of the head. Drill another hole into the neck and reconnect the two parts with a correct length of pin. You can then reposition the head, twisting or bending it into a new attitude. You can rebuild both head and neck into almost any configuration, combining your imagination with generous amounts of A+B putty.

CHAPTER THREE: CONVERTING

An alternative is to modify the existing Historex head without removing it from the neck. Cut a series of three or four notches into the outside of the existing neck, cutting almost all the way through the neck to allow you to gently bend it into position. If it breaks, super-glue the assembly back together and complete the positioning. The most important priority is to get the position correct at this stage. Strengthen and stabilize the final position with Five Minute epoxy and then fill the gaps with A+B putty, letting the entire assembly dry overnight. Add more putty and file the neck to final shape. The new assembly can then be glued with liquid plastic cement to the horse's body. If you add a drop of super-glue in the center and surround the area with the liquid plastic cement, you can continue working while the assembly dries. Add more A+B putty to make a smooth transition from the body to the new neck, creating the neck muscles as described above.

If the horse's height is to be increased, sever the lower legs just below the fetlock. Drill a

"Corporal, Ogilvy's Regiment" by Roger Becker, constructed from Historex parts, has a most purposeful trudge.

Dr Mike Thomas, Great Britain:

"I made my first Historex figurine about 25 years ago. It was a Sapeur of the Foot Chasseurs of the Imperial Guard; it took me about a day to assemble and paint; and it was awful! At the time, however, I thought it was great, and I quickly acquired more and more. My first mounted figure was a Polish Guard Lancer, and this one took

"Trumpeter, Polish Lancers of the Imperial Guard" by Dr Mike Thomas.

longer: three days. From that point on I have been hooked. I suppose that over the years I must have made a couple of hundred or so Historex models. So what was the attraction?

"Primarily it was the detail, the absolute fidelity (as I later discovered when I visited the Army Museum in Paris) of the engraving right down to the actual oak-leaves on a Marshal's coat, or the eagles on his baton. Once assembled, you had the feeling that what you had made was a real representation of the actual person. To be sure, there were faults: the Historex engravers never did succeed in cracking the problems of making hands that looked right, and that actually gripped a sword or musket, much less held the horse's reins properly. . .

"Then there were the horses - beautiful animals. Yes, I know they were more like thoroughbred Arabian steeds than the average cavalry mount; but the fact that you could make up practically hundreds of different horses by choosing different combinations of halves and heads made them a godsend for the modeller. With a little care it was always possible to 'improve' on things by making the horse wider.

"I quickly found that if I merely put the kit together from the packet what I got was a rather wooden-looking squaddie (a.k.a. "grunt"). Armed with my trusty pyro-gravure, razor saw and files it didn't take too much effort to create a more relaxed pose, or to turn a rider in the saddle. With more confidence came riders mounting, dismounting, or falling off horses in all sorts of unlikely attitudes. Great fun!

"There now opened up the whole field of conversions. The spares service run by Historex Agents under the inestimable Lynn Sangster at Dover meant that I could order swords, legs, heads, horse parts or what-have-you by return of post. You want to make Scots Highlanders? No problem. Indian Army cavalry? Easy. Knights in armour? Fine. It wasn't quite that simple, of course, but the potential was there, and finding out how to do it was great experience. Even today, when the quality and fidelity of metal figurines can equal those of injection moulded polystyrene, I will often rather reach for the Historex parts box.

"In the early days many experienced modellers, brought up on metal castings, tended to believe that plastic was cheap and cheerful; they preferred what they called the 'heft' of a 'real' figure. I never had this particular hang-up: once the paint was on it was impossible to tell the difference by looking - except, of course, that the detail was better.

"What else? The cost - always reasonable when compared to the price of a metal figure. Also, the way that the plastic took paint was a point in their favour. I have tried a variety of mediums, including gouache and acrylics, but my favourite remains artists' oils. There was so much detail on a kit that it cried out to be given a careful paint job; why, in the early days I could easily spend a whole evening just painting a horse, or a set of drum banners. . .These days a mounted figure will take me from six to eight weeks to complete. Now, you tell me where I can get that much fun, for that long a time, for less than 15 pounds."

CHAPTER THREE: CONVERTING

(Left) This wounded French Lancer by Shep Paine directs our eyes at once by his realistic concentration on the rag bandage held convincingly between his teeth. Another realistic campaign touch is the hooking up of the shabraque corner to protect its embroidery from mud and thorns.

(Right) "La Garde meurt et ne se rend pas!", Dave Peschke's tribute to the last moments of the Old Guard at Waterloo, features six modified Historex Grenadiers in a very effective grouping illustrating the advantages of tight composition. His careful animation work has entirely removed the somewhat wooden impression of standing Historex figures assembled straight out of the packet.
(Photo Lane Stewart)

CHAPTER THREE: CONVERTING

(Left) Fernand Backaert freezes the moment of combat in his "Dragoon and Lancer".

hole approximately 1/4in up into the leg and another through the hooves. Using a length of pin, reconnect the hooves and raise the overall height. Super-glue the assembly together and fill the gaps between the hooves and legs with putty. If you're creating a very large horse, build up the fetlocks to increase their bulk.

If you are further modifying the horse's legs, consult your references again to be certain of the pose. You have to know what a horse's legs will and will not do when moving or standing. To modify the position, remove the rear of the joint using a combination of wedge cuts and pyrogravure surgery at the joints. The removed sections can be filled by melting scrap plastic with the pyrogravure (a very strong joint) and then reshaped with putty. If the new leg position bears weight, you may have to remove it entirely and insert a length of pin for additional strength.

For dramatic effects, Historex horses can be poised on one or two legs. While the figure will not bend due to weight, it will be in danger of breakage since the lower leg is very thin. The leg can be rebuilt to ensure a stronger structure. Before assembling the body halves, rout out the inside surface of one supporting leg. Use a very small dental burr to cut a trench along the inside of the leg from the hoof to inside the body half. Bend a length of steel hobby (piano) wire until it fits inside the trench, leaving about 3/4in protruding from the hoof. Extend the other end up into the body cavity. Use Five Minute epoxy to glue the wire into place, liberally adding glue inside the body cavity to ensure a strong fit. When cured, fill the trench with A+B putty, re-sculpting the

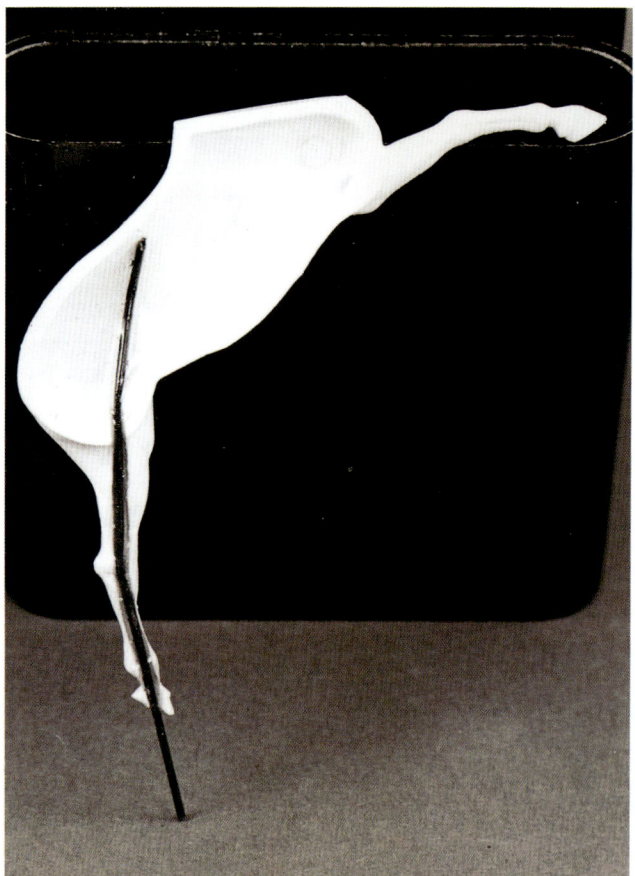

(Above) For a horse which will be posed with only one hoof touching the ground, reinforcement can be incorporated at an early stage by cutting a trench up the inside of that leg and cementing a length of steel wire in place with epoxy; note that the wire extends well inside the body cavity, where it can be generously anchored with epoxy. Once this is dry the visible surface of the leg can be reshaped using A+B putty.

CHAPTER THREE: CONVERTING

Joe Berton, USA:

"I grew up building model airplanes and ships. The skill was in following the detailed directions and making sure that you did not have any parts left over. At the age of fourteen I bought my first Historex kit, a mounted officer of the Chasseurs of the Guard. You can imagine my surprise and difficulty in identifying the parts, struggling with the French instructions and just trying to figure out where all the parts went. It was a rather feeble and frustrating struggle; I went back to working with Bussler kits, and saved my allowance to buy a Stadden.

"Marshal Ney" by Joe Berton.

"A year or so later I got involved with a local club, the Military Miniature Society of Illinois. A few of the modellers were doing wonderful things with Historex. Shep Paine, then a student at the University of Chicago, would show up at the monthly meetings with his latest creations; the rest of us, working with Rose, Stadden and I/R castings, would be amazed at the life he put into his figures. Then Shep started a painting class, and that led some of us away from bottled paint and into oils and mixing colours; and soon afterwards he took some of his graduates into a Historex class. Under his guidance we realized that we didn't have to use all the many pieces, nor were we limited to the pieces that came in that particular kit. Mix and match, cut it up and glue it, heat it and bend it - and pretty soon we were doing serious conversion work.

"We were all young, enthusiastic, and having so much fun. Every month some of us would put our latest Historex figures on display. We would share Historex lingo, use recently learned obscure French words for equally obscure military items, and discuss excitedly the latest releases of new subjects or spare parts. Our local hobby shop had an entire wall of Historex kits; Saturdays would find many of us in front of that display, just looking at parts and sharing ideas and techniques. Some of us were even asked by Lynn Sangster to participate in his latest Historex catalogue, and it was an honour to share space with the best in the hobby.

"Almost every month Shep would bring in another Historex piece that was eventually destined for his 'Eve of Essling' diorama. When Shep finally completed the diorama and displayed it, it caused a sensation. It was awe-inspiring; no miniature piece ever captured the modelling crowd like that one.

"Perhaps the best thing we gained from working with Historex was an ability to look at any kit or spare part and see the potential for something totally different. By mastering conversion techniques, we got rid of the notion of building the kit straight out of the box; every Historex model could be unique."

muscles, joints, hoof and fetlock by using an unmodified leg as a guide. The resulting new leg is very strong and not subject to breakage.

An additional impression of movement and action can be added to a galloping horse by laying its ears back along the head. If you look closely at photos you will see that the ears are reversed on many running horses. The conversion is relatively simple. In some instances the part can simply be reversed and tilted backwards. In other poses more radical ear surgery may be required. This involves cutting away both ears, leaving some extra plastic beneath them. Reverse them individually and glue each ear into the notch in the top of the head, making certain that they sit high enough on the head. Fill the gap around each ear with A+B putty, reshaping the skull. Most of this will later be covered by the forelock, but be certain that you have the correct shape.

A larger horse means a larger saddle. It is fairly simple to widen either a one-piece or a two-piece saddle. If it is the one-piece variety, use the razor saw to cut it in half from front to rear. The two halves can then be modified to

An early conversion of a Royal Scots Greys trooper by Shep Paine, carefully researched to include the standard field equipment of the 1815 Waterloo campaign in which the regiment earned immortality.

CHAPTER THREE: CONVERTING

A marvellous cavalry vignette by Andrei Koribanics, using Historex Carabiniers and Scots Greys and entitled "A Run for the Colour". Note that the five mounted figures are attached to the ground at only a few points, greatly increasing the illusion of movement. The close-ups show how Historex figures can be converted to interact closely with one another.
(Main photo Philip Stearns)

accommodate the wider horse. Drill two corresponding holes in the thicker area of both halves. Cut lengths of pin to insert into the holes, testing and recutting them until the saddle fits snugly over the horse's modified body. Glue the pinned assembly together, twisting and fitting it until the assembly fits against the horse's body. Fill the gaps between the saddle halves with scrap plastic and putty, pressing the saddle temporarily into place before the assembly dries to check for a good fit. Don't be too concerned at this point about the fit; just be certain that it fits reasonably close at the front, rear and sides. The front and rear gaps can be filled later.

Blanket rolls can be added underneath the raised pommel. Most Historex saddles portray this characteristic "hump" in front of the rider but fail to include the visible parts of the blanket. Roll out a thin sheet of A+B putty, letting it almost completely cure. Cut the small sheet of putty to shape and roll it up to simulate the blanket. Fit the two halves beneath the shabraque or saddle cloth, gluing them into place while the putty is still workable.

A+B putty can also be used to create new saddlecloths and shabraques as well as a variety of material. It is especially useful for creating cloth. First, make a paper pattern of the cloth item, test fit it, and put it aside for the moment. Mix slightly more putty than needed. Let the putty cure for 30 minutes or until it has lost most of its tackiness. Coat the inside of a plastic sandwich bag or two sheets of clear plastic with vegetable oil (or baby powder), and place the semi-cured lump of A+B putty inside. Roll it flat, reducing it to the proper thickness. Remove the putty, overlay the paper pattern as a guide, and cut the "cloth" into final shape using small scissors.

While still malleable, press the cloth pattern onto the figure or horse until satisfied that it drapes properly. Carefully remove it, add a drop of super-glue, and reattach the piece permanently into place. The major folds and wrinkles can then be gently pressed into the putty with toothpicks or similar tools, smaller areas being added later with putty. Don't be too concerned about the exact shape or condition of the added part at this point. Small tears or mistakes can be corrected with additional putty later.

Once the horse and saddle are completed, miscellaneous parts such as blanket rolls, valises, stirrups, etc. can be cleaned up and prepared for painting. Paint these early and set them aside to dry since they may require extensive handling later.

The author's "Chasseur Officer", built from standard Historex parts. The horse's head has been raised and the neck muscles rebuilt, while the tail has simply been reversed to simulate an abrupt halt.

Riders

Turning to the rider, first decide what position is to be recreated. Start with the legs first. Improve them by undercutting the boot tops, adding soles, and removing the spurs, mould lines and raised stripe details on each leg, which only get in the way of painting. Modify the leg positions if warranted by the pose. Replace the spurs with small lengths of insect pin.

Next, select the torso. Historex provide a variety of bodies with different uniform details and positions, some static and others in action poses. One of your conversion decisions concerns the uniform details. If you select a body to match your plan of a turning or leaning pose, it may not depict the correct uniform. However, with moderate effort you can scrape off the existing detail and resculpt the coat details.

Trial fit the legs to the body next. Experiment

CHAPTER THREE: CONVERTING

with different positions until you are satisfied with the pose. This may require a shim being added between the legs if the horse and saddle were widened. Attach the legs to the body. Don't be concerned with the exact fit at this point - it's more important to accurately create the pose you have in mind, and to make certain that it works. You may have to attach and disassemble these parts numerous times until you're satisfied with the positioning.

After assembly, the rider's seat will need adjustment. Place the rider in the saddle and check for a close fit. Add putty beneath the buttocks and inside the legs, wetting both the putty and saddle before pressing the rider into the saddle. Carefully remove the rider and allow the putty to cure. This will ensure a good fit as described earlier. File away any putty overlap. Next, temporarily fit both the saddle and the valise/blanket to check the fit of the coattails - chances are that they will need adjustment in order to drape properly.

The positioning of the arms plays a major part in conveying the action or mood being depicted, and problems arising when modifying and attaching the arms need to be resolved early. One concerns their length. Always check and recheck the converted "new arm" to ensure that you haven't inadvertently shortened or lengthened it. Check it against an existing part and recheck the new limb with a pair of dividers. The second area for particular care is raised arms. Too many times one sees a model arm which has been raised without regard to the consequent changes to the upper shoulder structure and the cloth covering it; these must be built up to accommodate the new arm position. Check and recheck the new positioning for length, folds and overall proportions.

Using existing Historex arms in conversions may require modifications. There are other very effective ways to convert figures, including building new limbs with a wire armature

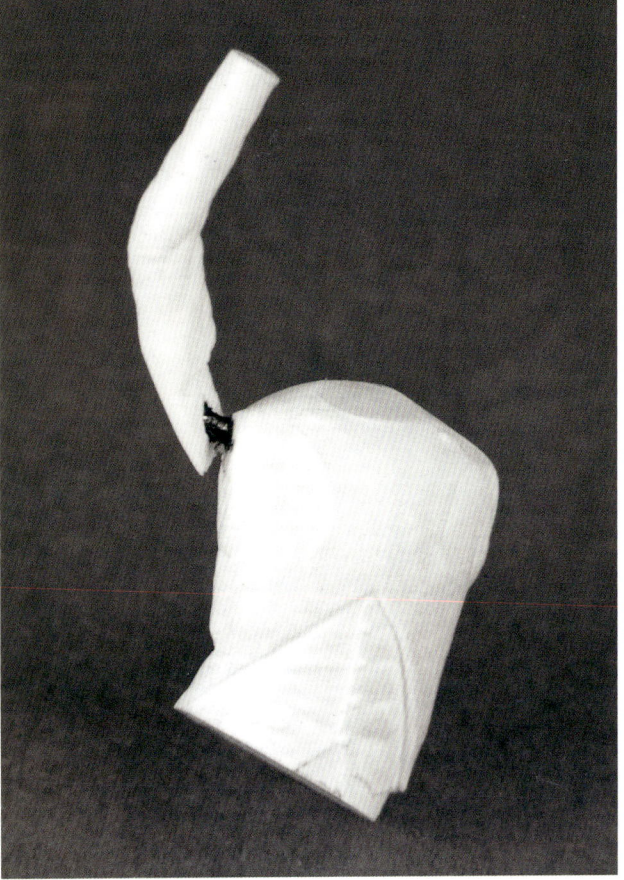

(Top) The fur colpak and feather plume were enhanced with the pyrogravure; the silver lace chevrons were painted onto the trousers and coat sleeves after removal of any moulded detail; and note the ricasso of the sabre blade, blued and decorated with gilding.

(Left) A raised arm also means that the entire shoulder area has to be raised. Note the pin positioning the arm, and that the arm has been lifted almost 1/8in. above the indicated location. New anatomy and uniform details will now be resculpted up to the notched area on the arm and in the armpit area.

CHAPTER THREE: CONVERTING

Two angles on a conversion to a "Hungarian Noble Guard" by Canadian master modeller Peter Twist, using modified Historex parts; note the strongly individual character of the face.
(Photo Lane Stewart)

and putty (see Bill Horan's book in this series); but I personally prefer to use existing Historex parts wherever possible.

It is critical to get the correct positioning, ignoring fit and neatness at the onset. I prefer to make the basic positioning changes before the arms are attached, test fitting their final positions. Next, drill out approximately 1/4in of the cuff area to accept the hands which will be inserted later. When satisfied with the final arm positions, use pins to attach the arms to the body. This allows you to check and recheck their positioning, bending the pin until you are satisfied with the pose. Look at the figure from all angles to be certain that it conveys what you had in mind.

Super-glue the pins and plastic into final position. Recheck the anatomy one final time to be certain that the dimensions are correct, and then fill the gaps with putty, modelling the arm into shape. If the finished arm just doesn't look right, don't be afraid to make additional modifications, even if it means removing the arm and starting over.

You should remember that modified arms, legs and other areas change the way the cloth wrinkles. I highly recommend the book *Dynamic Wrinkles and Drapery* by Burne Hogarth (Watson-Guptil Publishers, New York, 1992), which contains excellent illustrations indicating how cloth reacts in various situations. Adding folds and creases is usually done in two stages. The larger wrinkles are roughed in as major gaps are filled, by pressing the putty into position and then using a toothpick, insect pin or small rounded tool to lay in the creases. Additional or smaller folds can be added later with small strips of wet putty, faired into position with a wet brush. Where the wrinkles are curved, shape them using a wet brush. Don't be too symmetrical when adding folds and creases. Study how irregular these areas appear in real life; and remember that heavy cloth like woollen tunics or greatcoats will create different patterns of wrinkles than thinner materials like linen shirts or summer fatigue dress.

Add the head next, attaching it with a pin. This helps incorporate the head into final position: what is the head doing? Is it bent forward, backward or sideways? Should it be moved forward or backward in relation to the body? How will the collar be affected? Unnatural positioning of the head results in an awkward figure. Adopt the pose yourself in front of a mirror, and take time to study it.

Finally, add the headgear but don't attach the chin scales if they hang loose. They will interfere with painting the face and should be added after painting is completed. Assemble the rest of the figure, adding everything except weapons, loose straps, hands, or anything else which may make painting awkward - the golden rule for any assembly sequence.

CHAPTER THREE: CONVERTING

(Left) Yet another familiar but always popular Historex conversion by Shep Paine, "A Whiff of Grapeshot" was one of the first conversions to fully explore the possibilities of extreme animation. (Photo Lane Stewart)

(Right) "Sabres Wicked in Their Work" by the author, which includes converted Bavarian infantrymen and reworked French hussars.

(Below) "Battle of the Pyramids" by Joe Berton includes a reworked horse and Arabic rider as well as an extensively converted French infantryman. (Photo Lane Stewart)

(Opposite) This beautifully detailed conversion by Jerome Chaveau depicts a "Hussar of the Moldawsky Regiment". Both the uniform and the horse illustrate the extent of detail which can be accomplished with experience; remember that this photo shows the model some three times actual size - an unjustly merciless test. (Photo Dominique Breffort)

CHAPTER THREE: CONVERTING

CHAPTER THREE: CONVERTING

(Above left) Pierre Soulier's "Bonaparte Crossing the Alps" recreates the David painting of the same name. This was judged Best of Show at Hyères, 1995. (Photo Dominique Breffort)

(Above) "Carabinier Officer" by Ivo Preda, recreating a painting by Benigni reproduced on a *Uniformes* magazine cover. (Photo Dominique Breffort)

(Left) "Chasseur in Difficulty" by Christian Legros, catching the interaction of a foot figure and a mounted cavalryman, won a Bronze Medal at the Paris Mondial, 1996. (Photo Dominique Breffort)

CHAPTER THREE: CONVERTING

(Right) A subject which the author always wanted to recreate, and finally did: "Trumpeter, Artillery of the Guard" sounding the advance at full gallop.

(Left) "The Sergeant's Mare" by Shep Paine uses Cuirassier stable dress to good effect. It may seem obvious, but inexperienced modellers often fail to realise the visual importance of doing a little research to match the subject's order of dress plausibly with his activity.

(Right) A quiet pastoral scene, "Sleeping Hungarian" by Peter Twist - a delightful reminder that military subjects can also be depicted in serene moments, and another example of Twist's skill in facial animation. (Photo Lane Stewart)

CHAPTER THREE: CONVERTING

(Above) An old ceremony carried forward into today's military tradition: "Wetting the Stripes" by Shep Paine, which made use of three Historex Old Guard Grenadiers in a vignette depicting celebration of a promotion.

(Below) A grim little vignette inspired by a Gerry Embleton painting, in which Shep Paine realistically depicted a less glamorous aspect of the period: "Spoils of War, Spain 1810".

CHAPTER THREE: CONVERTING

(Above left) This detail - again, of a face smaller than your little fingernail - from Max Longhurst's "Grenadier à Cheval of the Guard" provides an excellent example of the character and expression which can be created with Historex heads.

(Above) By contrast, Jerry Hutter's "French Officer of the Line, 1800" is a simple foot figure reworked into a more convincing stance than the rigidity of the stock figure. Notice the careful handling of the stripes, the torn breeches and added scarf.

(Left) "Carabinier Trumpeter" by David Stokes depicts a colourful transition-period uniform. (Photo Phil Kessling)

CHAPTER THREE: CONVERTING

(Left) An early conversion and boxed diorama by Shep Paine, appropriately entitled "Idylls of the Voltigeur", needs little explanation.

(Below left) "Death Hussar" by Rob Baker, a very nicely finished stock figure.

(Below) Rob Baker's "Hussar", imaginatively set in an unusual but carefully animated pose rarely seen. This is an excellent example of a creative setting in limited space.

(Right) The drama and motion of "Capturing the Eagle" is recreated by Bill Pritchard in this Historex conversion.

(Opposite below left) Graham Brown's "Cleaning Equipment" is an effective presentation of a single figure.

(Opposite below right) "Chasseur à Cheval of the Guard in Winter Dress" by Dr Mike Thomas creates a simple but pleasing effect of windy weather by the angles of the colpak plume and bag, the cape and the horse's tail.

CHAPTER THREE: CONVERTING

CHAPTER THREE: CONVERTING

(Above left) The author's "Drunken Drum Major" was an experiment in balance. The bottom of the mace was drilled out and an insect pin was inserted; this also formed the right index finger, making a surprisingly strong attachment point. (Photo Bill Horan)

(Above) "Dear Jacques", Greg DiFranco's ironic depiction of an experience which has plagued soldiers through the ages, is a combination of both Historex and Airfix parts. (Photo Phil Kessling)

(Left) Ron Wehrman's stumbling "Drunken Carabinier", struggling with a recalcitrant horse, illustrates rather less elegant effects of self-indulgence than the dancing Drum Major...

CHAPTER THREE: CONVERTING

(Left) This "French Napoleonic Artillery Officer" by Graham Bickerton succeeds in creating a sense of urgency and arrested motion as the horse is reined hard back on the brink of a destroyed bridge.

(Below) "Officer, King's German Legion Heavy Dragoons" by the author shows the wear and tear on both man and equipment during Wellington's Spanish campaigns. Note the extensively converted pose, the repaired saddle and patched overalls, the enlarged bicorne and chinscales sculpted from A+B putty, the plume in a protective cover, the canteen with stopper and cord, and the resculpted hands. Note also, on the horse's near shoulder, the brand - a detail too often forgotten when painting military mounts.

CHAPTER THREE: CONVERTING

(Aove) This "Carabinier General" by the author incorporates a converted resin head which started life as a German SS officer - it has a properly arrogant stare for one of Napoleon's immortals!

(Left) "British Dragoon", a charming vignette by American modeller Barry King, won a medal at the 1996 Chicago show. (Photo Phil Kessling)

CHAPTER THREE: CONVERTING

(Above) Two contrasting aspects of the Emperor's cavalry by J-P.Duthilleul: a nicely animated "Commandant, 5th Hussars", and a foraging "Hussar in Spain".

(Left) Joe Berton's exciting conversion "Mamelukes in Egypt, 1799".

CHAPTER FOUR
PAINTING

"Dutch Lancer" in campaign dress by Shep Paine; note the sense of motion given by the excellent animation of the cantering horse's legs, and the angle as mount and rider lean into a corner.

Once the figure is assembled it is time to break out the paintbrushes. This is a critical phase, because there is a natural inclination to rush completion. After all, building and/or converting takes time. It's been a long process - cutting and filing, attaching many small pieces, working with putty, liquid sprue and various glues; now you are eager to get on with the painting so that the final appearance of the model, which you have held in your head for days or even weeks, can begin to emerge before your eyes. It is a real challenge to summon up the patience to lavish proper attention on the work you have put into the figure, and on the wealth of detail provided by Historex.

Don't rush this vital final step, hurrying the painting process in order to see the finished figure. There is no shortcut and no way to make up for weaknesses in painting or lack of attention to details. As in any scale, there are certain tricks of the trade; Historex offers its own set of challenges, but rewards careful painters with a true miniature if they are willing to devote the extra time. I've been asked many times how I paint the detail and rich colour, and my answer is always the same: very slowly and carefully. . . I wish that I could say there is some magic formula to speed the process, but there isn't.

This chapter hopefully shares a few more ideas for painting not just Historex but any small scale figures. Some of what follows may seem somewhat esoteric, but too many times one sees a Historex figure which "falls flat". The figure may appear very ordinary, and you may indeed need to look twice before realizing that it is a Historex at all. Lifeless figures generally result from an inability to make the figure "jump" - the failure to breathe life into all the detail and animation that's been created. The figure may look flat from too little shading or highlighting, or the colours may be drab, muddy or washed out. This may be due to inexperience, or to a failure to rethink painting in a smaller scale. Producing that added dimension may mean adjusting your usual painting style to accommodate both the scale and the degree of detail.

Painting styles vary dramatically; there is no right or wrong method, and I do not advocate one over another - whatever gives the best results for each individual is the "best" technique. My own style has been called everything from "Metro Goldwyn Mayer Technicolor" to "colourful and dramatic"; it's all in the eye of the beholder, and depends upon what the painter is trying to accomplish. He may be striving for the subtle yet detailed effect which Bill Horan, Jim Holt and Derek Hansen have mastered; or he may opt for the brighter distinction typical of the works of Phil Kessling, Mike Hall or Bob Knee. All of these painters' approaches are successful and they all bring life to the figure.

Positive results in this scale come from an increased awareness that the painter must be, for lack of a better term, more dramatic than

CHAPTER FOUR: PAINTING

Dennis Yieder's "The Skirmish" incorporates six foot figures in a very realistic Voltigeur vignette, which makes good use of terrain to accentuate the "story" behind the scene.

when working in larger scales, but without being coarse or creating a doll-like appearance. The smaller scale demands that you are doubly aware of detail and contrasts, of shading and highlighting. The potentially jewel-like appearance of a well painted Napoleonic uniform at this small scale is part of its charm; but to realize that potential demands as much, if not more work than in larger scales. The eye needs to be drawn into the fine array of detail provided by Historex. When the model is painted with care and patience, the spectator is immediately dragged forward into the scene being presented.

Paint selection

There is no single type of paint that can be labelled the "best" for painting miniature soldiers. Every medium from watercolour to sign paint has been used successfully to some degree. The only important factor is the end result. The three paints now dominating the scene are acrylics, enamels and artist's oils. My personal preference is for artist's oils, but only because they produce the final appearance I am seeking.

My two personal favourites are the Winsor & Newton and Liquitex lines. I also have a weakness for experimenting with other brands and new colours; despite the fact that I probably don't need them I enjoy testing new colours, so my paint drawer is filled with odd tubes. Although I like the Winsor & Newton brand, I have developed a special fondness for Liquitex oils, especially when painting Napoleonic figures. There is a brightness and crispness to Liquitex colours that I find attractive, combined with finely ground pigments and a relatively inexpensive price. I personally cannot distinguish any difference in quality in this less expensive line. If Liquitex has a weakness, it tends to have an excess amount of carrier (oil), which is inherent to some degree in certain colours of all brands - e.g. reds, greens, Ivory Black, etc. This is not a major drawback, however, and the "cure" discussed below even creates positive benefits in helping to produce a realistic finish.

Some observers have commented that my figures lack glossiness despite being painted with oils. There are several techniques to accomplish this effect. If the paint is too oily, turn the opened tube upside down onto a paper towel and gently squeeze out some of the excess carrier onto the paper. It may take several "purges" to remove much of the carrier in certain colours, and it may be necessary to repeat the process each time the paint is used. While this may reduce the paint's tube life, it does help reduce the oiliness.

You can also soak a small amount of the paint into paper or cardboard. Place a little more colour than you'll actually need onto an absorbent paper surface. Spread the paint to increase the absorption area and let it remain there for two to twelve hours, depending upon the oiliness. There is no magic formula for the amount of time; it's a learning process for each colour. After a few hours you'll see a ring of absorbed oil around the paint. If the paint still appears very wet, transfer it again to a dry area and continue soaking it. Be careful not to scrape too hard or you'll end up with unwanted

CHAPTER FOUR: PAINTING

Ron Wehrman took a page from Osprey's *Napoleon's Marshals* as his basis for this recreation of the wounding of Marshal Suchet at Sagunto. Attending him are a trumpeter of the 13th Cuirassiers and an ADC in light cavalry dress.

bits of paper in the paint. When the paint has stiffened somewhat, transfer it to your palette.

I use a good grade of artist's turpentine for mixing and thinning paint; it's more expensive, but I don't use large quantities and I find that it has two desirable traits. First, my experience has been that good turps tends to further reduce glossiness, and second, that colours seem to retain their brightness. Other mediums can dull a colour and the mixing properties may not be as good. I've also had good experience using Grumbacher Painting Medium I, which imparts a semi-matt finish. If all else fails, a thinned coat of Polly-S Matt Finish can be applied over thoroughly dry oils. It has an inherent advantage in that it can be selectively applied to small problem areas, avoiding the necessity of overspraying the entire figure. I've never found an area that could not be matted by using this product.

Another mixing medium which I find useful is Winsor & Newton's "Winton Painting Medium". This is especially useful if soaking the paint leaves it too dry for easy application after several days on your palette. Adding small amounts to the paint improves the flow and consistency and "re-wets" the paint for smoother application.

One final word on glossiness. Don't be overly concerned about creating a totally matt figure. Different cloths and materials impart different tones, some of which are dead matt while others have a slight sheen. Much of it depends upon material, age, dirt, degree of wear, etc. In fact, a completely matt figure is not realistic or accurate.

One of the really appealing aspects of oils is their versatility. There is virtually no end to the richness of colour that can be created. Oil paints are easily mixed to create warm or cold colours, bright or subdued tones, parade ground prettiness or field scruffiness. They also dry more slowly, permitting very subtle shading and highlighting.

Many other painters are surprised that I also prefer oils when it comes to painting fine detail, rather than the acrylics which are popular for such work. Painting details is almost an art unto itself in this scale. As most experienced painters know, it is the consistency, not the type of paint, which is critical in determining how easily details can be painted. Unless you learn to thin the paint to its proper state of viscosity (which Shep Paine likened to that of "warm butter"), excess paint application will obscure details, cause build-up problems, and generally result in a poorly painted figure. An inability to maintain the proper consistency can often be traced simply to an unwillingness to continuously remix the paint on the palette to maintain the proper flow from the brush to the model. If the correct viscosity is maintained *throughout the entire painting process* then shading and highlighting, as well as the finest detail work, is easily accomplished with oils. But the painter has to overcome the natural tendency to "work just a little longer with this hour-old dab of paint" without thinning or remixing it.

CHAPTER FOUR: PAINTING

Historex's "Field Forge" is shown here in use, repairing a Gribeauval 8-pounder; for scale, Larry Munné has incorporated a soldier performing another unavoidable task...

Preferred tube colours are a matter of individual taste. Everyone has a list of favourites; my own include:

Winsor & Newton	*Liquitex*
Titanium White	Unbleached Titanium
Ivory Black	Mars Black
Blue Black	Neutral Gray Value 5
Naples Yellow	Permanent Indian Yellow
Chrome Yellow	Hansa Yellow Medium
Mars Yellow	Cadmium Red Medium Deep
Cadmium Yellow Deep	Cadmium Red Medium Light
Mars Orange	Medium Portrait Pink
Mars Brown	Mars Orange
Burnt Umber	Brilliant Blue
Burnt Sienna	Cerulean Blue
Bright Red	Permanent Light Blue
Cadmium Red	Emerald Light Green
Indian Red	Metallic Silver
New Blue	
Prussian Blue	
Chrome Green	

One note regarding the Liquitex Neutral Gray Value 5: it's an excellent tinting medium to reduce the chromo (brightness) in a colour which may appear too stark or unrealistic. Adding minute amounts of this "colour" means that you are adding a small amount of black and white, thereby reducing the brightness without drastically affecting the basic colour.

Brushes are always a favourite topic among painters. Like most experienced painters, I prefer the Winsor & Newton Series 7 red sable brushes; I also use the Grumbacher 178 Series line of sables. There are other good brushes, but the consistency of these lines is unexcelled. I do not use the cheaper synthetic brushes: they look great in the art store, but the tip loses its point very quickly, curling into an unusable hook after a few sessions. If you're serious about painting quality figures, spend your money on good brushes and take care of them. This is more important than you might think, since painting figures and repeated cleaning is rough on brushes. Insofar as size is concerned, very fine detail can be painted with a good No.1 or 0 sable brush. I rarely use anything smaller than a 000 size, simply because very small brushes don't hold enough paint and don't last.

The **undercoating** process is very important. Oil paints are either translucent or opaque by nature, depending upon the colour. The covering power of specific colours will vary; knowing which oils cover well and which are semi-transparent is part of the learning process. Since Historex figures are white styrene, covering power is critical. Undercoating with a water-based paint provides two benefits: the painting surface is changed from stark white to the approximate final colour, and the water-based paint will not be lifted by subsequent applications of turpentine, oil paints or petroleum-based paint thinners. I prefer to undercoat using the Polly-S line of acrylics, which are easily thinned and provide a smooth painting surface. Matching the exact final oil colour is not as important as an even undercoat applied in one or two very thin coats. Be careful not to get carried away with the undercoating

CHAPTER FOUR: PAINTING

process or you'll obscure much of the detail. Let the undercoat dry for at least 24 hours before over-painting with oils.

Every painter has a favorite **palette** on which to mix paint, ranging from glass, ceramic plates, 3x5 cards, newspapers, etc. My personal choice is freezer paper, specifically "Reynolds Freezer Paper (Plastic Coated)" which is available in your grocery store. Freezer paper has the advantage of one plastic-coated side while the reverse is a more porous surface. The coated side does not easily absorb paint which means that oils stay usable for longer periods. The other side also has its uses since it readily absorbs excess oil. Before taping a sheet to my work area I turn down a corner to expose some of the porous side, providing me with a handy area on which to soak small amounts of paint if necessary.

Mixing and remixing paint means that something has to be used to blend and thin it. I initially used the brush handle, ruined ten or fifteen shirts, and looked for alternatives. My best solution has been toothpicks; they are cheap, can be wiped relatively free of paint and re-used. Toothpicks are also handy for holding small parts for painting and various other small tasks.

Another question sometimes asked is how I can see the small detail. The answer is simple: I cheat. Since I am very farsighted I need help in magnifying the entire Historex figure. My solution has been to use the inexpensive eyeglasses which can be purchased in a drugstore (I'm told that they are now available in Britain from some large branches of Tesco, at less than three pounds). These simply magnify without correcting vision defects. I also use an "Optivisor" which is made especially for detail work, wearing it over the eyeglasses for additional magnification. Since I don't paint for long periods of time, I find that this works extremely well, allowing me to paint almost any detail, no matter how small, without tiring my eyes.

*   *   *

Before discussing the specifics of painting small details and equipment, there are several general considerations which affect the success

(Below left) Mike Thompson's "Kettledrummer, Gendarmes d Élite".

(Below) One of the Royal Scots Greys from Shep Paine's "Scotland Forever!"; note the corrected appearance of the bearskin headgear.

CHAPTER FOUR: PAINTING

or failure of smaller scales. The painter always needs to remember that smaller models do not mean less work or less attention to detail. As mentioned above, the appeal of these small scales lies in the realism which has been reproduced in miniature. If there is one hard-and-fast rule, it is this: the smaller the scale, the higher the degree of contrast required. The overall effect of a small figure may be weakened or altogether lost if the smaller parts lack definition, crispness and subtle contrast.

Creating the appropriate contrast begins with an understanding of how light affects the final appearance of surfaces. The light source is either dictated (as in a boxed diorama) or implied by painting (a freestanding figure). When painting the latter you must first decide where the imagined source of light will be in relation to your model; and then paint it to display shadows and highlights according to the dictates of this constant factor. The resulting "cone of light" determines where each colour will be applied. (Although it deals specifically with flat painting, there is much which "round" modellers will find valuable in the relevant chapter of Mike Taylor's *The Art of the Flat Tin Figure*, Windrow & Greene, 1995.)

If the light source is above the figure - most obviously, during a bright summer's day - then highlights will naturally fall on the shako top, upper shoulders, upper surfaces of the arms and legs, boot top edges, upper ridges of folds, etc.; shadows, accordingly, would be applied to such areas as the underside of the arms, legs, creases and folds. The degree and intensity of highlights and shadows are ruled by common sense and the laws of nature, both of which require some study before starting to paint. How prominent is the crease's ridge? Should the highlight colour be stark in contrast (a sharp fold), or subtle (a gentle rise in the cloth)? How deep is the fold - should the shadow be very dark or just a hint? Bear in mind that highlights and shadows are not applied simply to the inner and outer general surfaces, but rather to the tops of the ridges and the undersurface of the recesses. Even minute areas need to follow the rules of the implied light source for an appearance of consistency.

The more "extreme" or unusual the implied light source, the more care is required to get

(Above) A Carabinier brushing out his bearskin, a quiet but convincing pose by Larry Munné.

(Left) "West India Regiment" by Peter Twist, a Historex conversion with rebuilt arms in a very natural pose.

CHAPTER FOUR: PAINTING

Shep Paine's "Cuirassier Trooper" features a helmet crest made from crepe hair.

the painting hand against it. This provides a steady platform for painting, while the figure can be held comfortably for long periods of time. Just be certain that the temporary base permits you to brace your painting hand: freehand, unbraced detail painting is a guarantee of frustration and poor results.

Painting the face and flesh

Once the model is attached to the temporary base, I begin by painting the face. The process starts with a very thin undercoat of Polly-S Midstone. I let this dry for at least 24 hours and then begin painting with oils. The eyes are probably the most important feature and will affect the entire figure, since the viewer's eye is first drawn to the face. I use oils exclusively to paint the eyes since I find them easier for painting fine detail; but years of experience led to this personal preference, and acrylics or enamels will work just as well.

First, apply a thin off-white coat; this forms the eyeball. Let it dry. Next, add a dark blue or brown iris, being careful to make them equal size and equal distance from the nose - you cannot be too careful in making certain you get this right. If you are aiming for a sideways, upward or downward glance, check the iris size and spacing carefully. If you're into completely realistic detail you can add a minute black pupil in the centre of the iris, but it's not really required since only a minimum of this area is visible. You can, however, give one final touch of realism by adding a minuscule "catchlight" reflection to the pupil or iris with the tiniest speck of white paint.

Since Historex figures have finely engraved eyes, it's relatively easy to paint them if you take your time. If you're not satisfied, start the process all over. If you make a mistake it's easy to remove the paint and begin again.

Paint the recessed eye socket next, using the medium shadow colour of Burnt Sienna or Indian Red. This includes the upper eyelid and the area immediately beneath the eye, reducing the outlines of the eyeball, and even further reducing both eyelids. Be careful of extremes in both areas; if not carefully reduced the figure will appear to be wearing mascara, while too little outline renders the eyes indistinct. Find a happy medium by carefully studying photos, and the people around you.

Once you're satisfied with this first stage of painting the eyes, you can then begin painting the face while the area is drying. Everyone has a favourite flesh tone formula and the final

your idea across visually. Supposing that your model is an "after the battle" vignette of a weary figure on a stricken field, then a successfully implied light source consistent with the strong, low-slanting beams of sunset will add greatly to the desired effect (and may also govern your exact judgement of colour mixes). A figure presented in a snowy scene will demand quite different handling. This sort of painting requires careful thought and a lot of practice, but can repay high dividends in its immediate visual impact.

It goes without saying that an absolute must for painting in any scale is a stable temporary base. The figure should be mounted so that both hands can have access; it must also be easily removable when completed. For years I have used several 5in cardboard tubes for this purpose. These are almost solid cardboard and fit the hand perfectly. Their thickness allows them to be easily drilled to accept mounting pins. Best of all, they are long enough to allow holding the figure in one hand while bracing

CHAPTER FOUR: PAINTING

Three models by Dr Mike Thomas: "Poniatowski", "ADC to Marshal Soult", and "Kettledrummer of the Empress Dragoons".

Titanium White should be used very sparingly to tint the basic flesh tone, as discussed below. Burnt Umber is used very sparingly for deep shading, although care is needed to avoid dragging this colour into other painted areas; since it contains black it will muddy everything it touches unless carefully controlled and contained in small areas.

Once the flesh tone is mixed, I first rough in the remaining medium shading with minute amounts of Burnt Sienna or Indian Red. These areas include cheek depressions, beneath the lower lip, beneath the chin and jawline, the temples, creases beneath the sides of the nostrils, the outline of the ears, the outline of all hair, beards and moustaches, the sides of the nose, and where the headgear meets the forehead or hairline.

While these areas are still wet, add the medium highlight colour - the basic flesh tone lightened with Titanium White and a touch of Bright Red. It is applied to the ridge of the nose, the nostril pads, the upper chin area, the tops of the ears and earlobes, the upper cheekbones, the ridges over the eyes, the area above the temples, and the jawline. Remember to add only very small amounts of paint; avoid overlapping the colours, blending only the adjoining edges.

selection depends upon personal preference to some degree. Remember that soldiers spend most of their time outside, so their skin tones will be darker than the office workers most of us see every day. My favourite basic mix is:
  Naples Yellow (50%)
  Burnt Sienna or Indian Red (25% to 40%)
  Portrait Pink (5% to 10%)
  Bright Red (1%)
  Burnt Umber (minute amounts for deep
    shading only)
  Titanium White

To paint the mouth, add a small touch of Bright Red to the medium highlight colour -

CHAPTER FOUR: PAINTING

(Above left) "Guard Grenadier Kettledrummer" by Bill Liebold.

(Above) "Mounted Chasseur" by Pierre Conrad.

(Left) Joe Berton's "Murat in Egypt" combined a Historex figure with a modified Breyer's "toy" horse.

(Opposite) This scouting British trooper in the 1812 pattern uniform of the "11th Light Dragoons", by Bill Horan, includes a Historex horse and some Historex equipment with an almost totally scratchbuilt rider, all painted in his inimitable style. (Photo Bill Horan)

not too much, or you'll produce a lipstick look. If the mouth is open, paint the inside with a dark red; if teeth are present, outline them with Burnt Umber and then use pure white to paint them. An open or closed mouth requires patience to achieve the right look, so take your time.

Next, fill in the remaining unpainted facial areas with basic flesh tone. As small as these areas of the three shades are (medium shade, medium highlight, and basic flesh tone), you

CHAPTER FOUR: PAINTING

should blend them as delicately as possible without losing the contrast. Blend the edges of all three very carefully with a *dry* brush. If you use a wet brush you will re-thin the paint and the blending process will remove too much paint, retarding rather than enhancing the desired blended effect. A separate brush which is totally dry allows you to gently pull the three areas together in a smooth transition. Using the smallest possible amount of paint will prevent an unwanted build-up. Smaller scales do not require much paint and the undercoating precludes the need of heavy applications of oils. A good rule is to reduce the amount of paint you think you'll need by at least half.

After you have applied and blended these three basic colours, let the paint dry overnight. Resist the temptation to continue - if you go on painting too long the paint will build up, and you'll have what Stan and Ollie called "another fine mess!"

Even when partially dry, you'll notice that the face still does not seem alive at this point; it looks acceptable, but rather bland. This is especially noticeable in smaller scales, where deeper shadows and more dramatic highlights still need to be added. At this point I begin the process of adding two new sets of shadows and highlights.

Begin with the medium shading colour, slightly darkened by a touch of Cadmium Red Deep, Mars Brown, or Violet. This colour is used to deepen the areas immediately beneath the lower lip, the outline of the hair, beard and moustaches, any chin clefts, any "crow's-feet" wrinkles, and ear details. The area immediately beneath the cheekbones should also be shaded delicately with this colour, using it very sparingly. These minute applications are blended into surrounding colours with a dry brush so as not to lift your previous work.

The final shading step is a still deeper shadow, added with Burnt Umber in *extremely* minute amounts, and taking great care not to let this mixture muddy the other colours. This deepens the areas that require additional shading: under the nose, the sides of the nostril pads, the inner ear, the division of the lips, and the inside corners of the eyes. This is probably the most delicate task of all, since overdoing it can make the face appear doll-like and coarse. What you are seeking is subtlety, not an array of hard contrasting lines.

The next step is to add the lighter highlights. The crispness of Historex engraving lends itself to this stage of painting. Again, there are two stages for applying these highlights. First, let your work to this point sit untouched until the face is three-fourths dry; this may add an extra

Martin Livingstone, Great Britain:

Martin Livingstone's "General de Brigade des Cuirassiers, 1805".

"I've always believed that 'Historex artists' have been a breed apart, especially those who produce mounted pieces. There are any number of ways to enhance the basic mounted figure - reworking the horse's head with A+B putty, creating a new bridle and bridoon from plastic strip, or reworking the mane, tail and forelock with Duro putty. The best thing for me when converting Historex is the ease with which extreme animation can be achieved, due to the lightweight plastic (which can be further strengthened by inserting wire supports where necessary).

"Many of my conversion techniques were originally developed by Ray Anderson. I soon learned to soften plastic card with solvent, allowing it to become partially dry so that it was less tacky, but soft enough to be malleable. My figures' clothing patterns were those included with the Historex Academy figures, using facial tissue and liquid plastic [sprue] to form the clothing itself. Details were added with thickened liquid sprue using a sable brush. The main disadvantage to this method is the slowness due to the solvent's evaporation rate, not to mention the risk to one's health! Although I now use a variety of putties, there are times when I prefer to use tissue and liquid plastic for items such as silk sashes and lace collars on 17th century gentlemen. I have also driven myself crazy using nylon stocking material and liquid plastic to create mail armour!

"I have been converting Historex since 1979, and I still enjoy producing mounted pieces. However, I've found increasing pressure to exceed the quality of each successive piece, and to try to keep up with fellow artists. I believe that Historex has made the most serious contributions as a medium to the current standards seen in competitions. Artists are constantly pushing the limits forward, and the French artists of the 1980s readily come to mind in this context. The end result is that I constantly look forward to each new show."

CHAPTER FOUR: PAINTING

day or two to the project, but be patient. Look at the original highlights which remain after the previous round of shading and blending. Once again you will notice that the face isn't quite alive. This is where the next round of highlighting pays dividends.

First, add a very small amount of Titanium White to the medium highlight colour to produce a still lighter highlight. Carefully blend small amounts into the highest points of existing highlighted areas with a dry brush. At this point you will begin noticing a certain new life in the face. This colour is also added as final touches to the eyes. Carefully paint the upper eyelids to define the eyes' shape; next, add the bags beneath the eyes, redefining their shape with the medium shading colour beneath each one, and blending this area carefully into the basic flesh tone.

Let the entire face dry completely before adding the following final highlights. Apply pure Titanium White in *extremely* minute amounts to the highest points of the cheekbones, the tip of the nose, the area immediately inside the creases which run from the sides of the nose downwards, the corners of the mouth, the upper temples, the area running from the upper sides of the nose diagonally beneath the bags under the eyes, and the very centre of the lower lip. The amount of pure white blended into these points is no more than a pinpoint of paint on the very tip of the brush. Blending them successfully requires no more than the lightest possible touch of the brush, being careful not to remove this white highlight in the process. Finally, add a very thin line of reflected light to the ridge above the upper lip - this is very discernible when you study how light strikes the mouth.

When painting the hair the overall shape of the mass of hair needs to be considered from the viewpoint of the light source. Shadows and highlights should be painted on and blended as variant shades of the chosen hair colour; the same applies to beards and moustaches.

Hands (and feet, in the case of a barefooted figure) also require the same attention. Like the face, hands are a critical focus of the spectator's attention; they are usually either grasping weapons, pointing, or expressing some phase of action, so the eye is drawn to them. Overcome the temptation to pass the paintbrush quickly over them. Creases need shading and knuckles should be highlighted. Fingers and hands should to be painted in accordance with the implied source of light. Even fingernails and prominent veins can be added with the lighter highlight colour.

"Trumpeter, 13th Regiment, 1802" by Jim Booth.

Outlining

In applying dark outlines to bring out details many painters go to extremes. Some even resort to using black as the outline colour, which results in a harsh, unnatural appearance. There is, however, a place for careful outlining; handled with care, it can serve as a way to bring details to the forefront. Certain areas literally beg for special attention if they are not to be lost. Examples include pockets, belting, buttons, cuffs, bridles and harnesses, insignia, decorations and medals, stripes, chevrons, etc. The trick to achieving a quietly effective success is colour selection. I find that as a general rule a darkened shade of the underlying colour works best. On a light blue tunic you would use a medium to medium-dark blue to outline the pockets; on khaki, a dark brown; on lighter reds, a dark red-brown, and so forth. The method of applying the outline is also important. Smaller parts such as buttons and medals need sharper definition which is created by a darker, crisper outline colour. Larger areas (pockets, belting) can be more subtly outlined, the result actually being more akin to shading but nonetheless distinct. This means carefully blending the outline colour into the surrounding areas. It's worth the effort to look critically at areas that can be enhanced and delineated by isolating them in outline form.

CHAPTER FOUR: PAINTING

(Right) An almost stock Historex figure of a "Cuirassier General" by Shep Paine.

(Left) A beautifully painted "Chasseur à Cheval de la Garde", by a modeller whose name is sadly lost to the author.

CHAPTER FOUR: PAINTING

Dry-brushing

If there is one general rule applying to dry-brushing, it is simply: don't do it! Too many painters believe that they have discovered a clever alternative to careful shading and highlighting - just put dark colours in the creases and drybrush a lighter shade over the ridges. The result is mediocre (if you're lucky); it will look as if you took a shortcut that didn't work. Like any rule, however, there are times when it can be broken. Dry-brushing works most effectively when you are trying to highlight very busy work such as a pyrogravured sheepskin shabraque, a heavily textured plume or groundwork. However, it is a process that requires discipline and practice; poorly applied, dry-brushing can be mistaken for sloppy or careless painting.

To begin dry-brushing, run a thin wash of the darkened basic colour onto the surface to be highlighted. When dry, you can begin the process. The first dry-brushed colour should be a slightly lighter shade. How carefully it is applied decides the degree of success. The trick is to pick up barely enough paint to adhere to a thoroughly dry brush, wiping off most of it on a paper towel. The residue left in the brush can then be lightly brushed over the very tops of the area to be highlighted, letting the surface "pull" the almost dry paint off the brush. Use fairly stiff paint, and don't wet your brush or pick up too much paint. If you do either you will over-paint the shaded area and will have to start over again. Once the initial highlight colour is dry, go back over the same area with a still lighter shade, barely touching the very tips of the affected areas again.

A detail from Shep Paine's "The Sergeant's Mare", an excellent illustration of a horse's open mouth which reveals the front teeth only.

Weathering

It's a matter of personal taste as to how much a figure should be weathered, or whether it should be "dirtied" at all. The painter needs to be aware of the setting, mood and groundwork around the figure. Is the subject on the parade ground or slogging across a rain-soaked field? Will Marshal Davout be presentable to the Emperor at an Imperial Review, or is he riding along a dusty summer road in Prussia?

The problem with choosing not to weather figures is that they can seem totally out of place in their setting. I remember putting hours of work into a piece I called "Sabres Wicked in Their Work" depicting three French hussars riding down several Bavarian infantrymen. The vignette was obviously a combat scene, but a judge pointed out that there wasn't a speck of dust or dirt on anyone involved. In retrospect I realized that all the effort put into three mounted figures and two heavily converted infantrymen was diminished because the whole scene looked too pristine. While I later added some weathering, it was a lesson well learned.

Weathering takes some forethought, patience and courage. The courage can be critical, since it is difficult for some painters to bring themselves to disrupt careful painting with mud and dust. If you want a rewarding experience, however, experiment by adding realistic touches to soldiers who live in the field. My technique is to first select those uniform parts obviously affected (trouser cuffs, knees, elbows, coat hems, boots, etc.), taking care not to forget the exact setting. With mounted cavalry don't neglect saddle cloths and shabraques, which should also show wear-and-tear. I add the appropriate mud, dust or weathered appearance into the base colour, painting the effect as

Mike Hall, USA:

"Like many, I was first introduced to Historex figures during the 1960s shortly after they became available in the United States. Peter Blum's Soldier Shop in New York and Valley Plaza Hobbies in North Hollywood, California, were the main suppliers. Being a somewhat unimaginative 'metal man', my first reaction to the Napoleonics produced in white plastic was similar to that of a witch-hunter in Colonial Salem - heresy! Plastic was meant for tank, airplane and ship model kits, not military miniatures. In short order I was proven very wrong, as the few periodicals of the time started publishing photographs of the works of Shep Paine, Max Longhurst, Pierre Conrad, and others. The figures they produced were stunning, and provided the initial impetus for me to acquire a 'great white plastic army' to complement the 'great grey metal army' I had on hand.

"When the first bagged cavalry figures arrived I was dismayed. I opened the bag, poured out the parts, carefully returned the parts to the bag, and thought 'maybe in the next lifetime'. The engraving of the parts was exceptional; but there were so many little pieces, I wondered how a mere mortal could be expected to assemble and paint an acceptable figure. It was approximately three months before I again opened a bag and laid out the parts. Overcome by curiosity, I started to clean up the mould lines, glue sub-assemblies together, and became so fascinated with what could be done that before I knew it, I had an assembled figure ready to paint. It wasn't nearly as difficult as I had thought, and it was fun.

"Historex had introduced a new medium to the hobby which broke new ground and, I believe, stretched the imagination of many modellers. This in turn has allowed the hobby to evolve and improve in a myriad of ways - including the introduction of resin casting. The hobby owes a lot to Historex."

Mike Hall's "Murat and Captain Manhés", a vignette of the cavalry commander and one of his aides at Eylau, 1807, after a plate by Chris Warner in the Osprey Men-at-Arms title Napoleon's Marshals.

I go, rather than overpainting a finished surface. It's very easy to go overboard, so understate the effects for better results; this is another case of "less is more".

For example, depending on the circumstances, mud can be either caked onto the lower trousers and coat hem, or limited to light stains, depending upon the season, ground and weather. Getting the right look depends upon selecting the right weathering colour to match the scene. In almost every situation the colour needs to be feathered into the base colour without harsh demarcation lines.

Pastel chalks can also be used, especially if the terrain of the selected groundwork is dry or dusty. Scrape off a little pile of colour from a pastel stick and apply the powder with an old brush; it will cling to the surfaces surprisingly like paint. Treat all weathering as you would any shading or highlighting. For the best examples of how to depict soldiers in the field, look closely at Bill Horan's work. His figures have a simple elegance to them which is not diminished by the application of Mother Nature's fingerprints.

Horses

Painting Historex horses is one of my favourite activities. The accuracy and moulding of their horses lend themselves to the paintbrush. If you're not familiar with equine colouring and anatomy, I suggest that you buy several of the kind of inexpensive picture books on horses usually found in the bargain section of any bookstore; you will find them invaluable guides for painting various types of horses. Study the photos, paying particular attention to the combinations of colours and to muscle definition.

As when painting the rider, the first step is to undercoat the horse. The approximate base colour should be thinly applied and allowed to dry overnight. Repeat if necessary to get good opaque coverage. Next, select the desired horse colour. The choice of a bay, chestnut, black, grey, or an anomaly such as a pinto or appaloosa (in British terminology, piebald or skewbald) is usually dictated by the subject. A little extra research can provide information about what colour should be selecte d. Did the regiment ride a certain colour of horse? Did officers as well as trumpeters ride greys? Were piebalds or skewbalds ever employed? Were there exceptions? Did locale or campaigning difficulties create unique exceptions to the regulations?

Another consideration is the difference in

CHAPTER FOUR: PAINTING

(Left & below) General view and detail of the author's "Engineer Officer", with reworked horse's mane, tail and forelock. The detail is perhaps a good example of the visual interest which can be created even with rather plain uniforms and accoutrements by careful shadowing and highlighting and crisp edges.

texture and the degree of gloss when comparing the horse to the rider. Too often one sees a good Historex piece marred by the fact that the horse's coat is as matt as the rider's tunic. Besides being inaccurate, the effect is totally incongruous. Except for greys, most horses' coats display a great deal of sheen; their hide contains natural oils, and they were regularly brushed and curried. Luckily, if you're painting in oils, the natural properties of such paints give an excellent approximation of a glossy coat, and oils used directly from the tube usually produce the desired sheen.

Once the horse colour is selected a thin coat is initially applied in several areas, beginning with the base colour and the highlight colour. The highlight should be added to the most prominent areas: the rump, neck and flank muscles, the leg muscles and the sides of the belly. I then fill in the remaining areas with

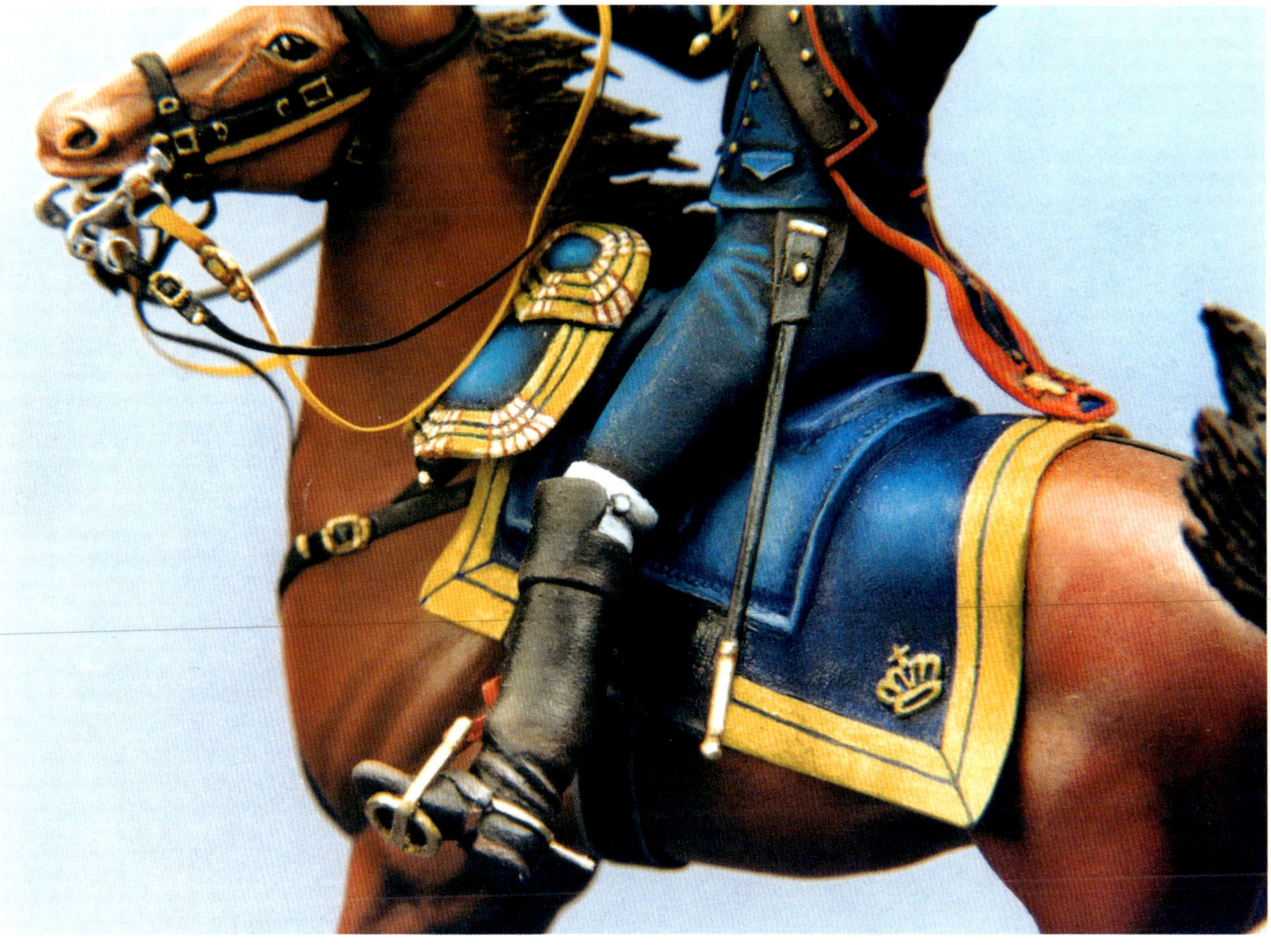

CHAPTER FOUR: PAINTING

The author's tranquil scene of a "Trumpeter, 6th Chasseurs à Cheval" taking a moment to converse with nature. The little bird was scratchbuilt, and minute holes were drilled into the rider's finger for its feet. Also observe the red and white trumpet cord; and the weathering on the horse's legs and belly as well as the rider's overalls.

The horse for the 20th Chasseurs trumpeter, fully painted and awaiting attachment of saddle and rider.

the base colour, and begin pulling the two shades together by blending with a dry brush - I save the shaded areas for later. Carefully feather the base and highlight colours together using a stippling, dabbing motion, blurring only the immediate areas where the colours meet. If you over-blend the two shades you'll end up with one colour.

Look at photos of the belly of the horse. It will often be a different colour, darker or lighter, depending upon the breed and colouring; and this area is also affected by the fact that it is always shaded from the light source to some degree. Next, add the shading colour to the various muscle groups, joints, lower neck, belly, around the harnessing and bridle bands, and beneath the tail. Blend this colour carefully into the surrounding base colour.

The first application of paint is now complete; but there is still room for improvement. When the paint is almost (or even completely) dry, final highlights can be added for better definition. Lighten the highlight colour still further and define the leg muscles, veins (belly and head), eye ridges, ear tips, nostrils, etc. Blend this colour carefully into the surrounding areas but keep it prominent enough to create distinct definition. A thinned wash of the shadow colour can also be applied to the recesses to augment these areas if necessary. This may seem like a prolonged process, but the end result warrants it. A well-painted horse is vital to the appearance of any good mounted figure.

Painting an all "white" horse (actually a grey) is a slightly different proposition. While the actual shade of grey can vary tremendously, one of the problems encountered is that white oil paints are very translucent. A solid, unbroken white undercoat is required. The subsequent shading and highlighting require slightly different techniques, given the properties of white paint. Firstly, never use pure white straight from the tube as the basic colour; if you do, you'll obviously have nothing left to use as a

CHAPTER FOUR: PAINTING

"Élite Gendarmes of the Guard" by Shep Paine.

Peter Twist, Canada:

Peter Twist's "Marshal Poniatowski". (Photo Lane Stewart)

"I was initially drawn to the Historex figures because of the exquisite detail and myriad of pieces that came with each kit. Since each figure had many extra parts on a sprue, conversion possibilities presented themselves immediately. After working on the first few of these plastic masterpieces, I also started to notice that the sculptor was using 'heroic' proportions which gave the kits an elegant appearance. At that time, in the late 1970s, most metal figures suffered from gigantic heads and shoulders, the rest of the sculpture being compressed to 'keep the figure in scale'. The beautifully shaped Historex pieces stood out immediately from the mass of mediocre product that was currently on the market.

"Converting plastic bodies was easily done using a fine razor saw and plastic wedges to change angles, and car spot putty restored the altered areas to a finished appearance. As I began to make more and more radical alterations, it became obvious that the extreme light weight and high strength of plastic made unbalanced poses easy to achieve: there was no metal fatigue, which could cause a cast metal figure to sag over time into a new and unwanted pose.

"Throughout the years Historex never failed to provide the same superb quality of sculpting and moulding, giving me the raw materials to create original subjects of my own."

highlight colour. Start with an off-white which can range from a light grey to a heavily dappled dark grey. Since grey tends to produce a drab effect, life can be added with the barest touches of pink or even blue to the base colour, being very careful not to overdo it. You can then use white straight from the tube for highlights.

The real challenge comes with the shading, which entails the smooth and subtle transitions from the light areas to deeper recesses. If you're not careful, over-emphasized shadowed areas will look like stripes. The shading needs first to be applied in relatively lighter tones than used for other colours, carefully blending this darker colour into the edge of the base colour. If the resulting shading is too light, very thin shading washes can be added in several gradual stages. As a final touch to smooth out these transition areas, washes of the base colour can be flowed into the shaded recesses to reduce the contrast. When totally dry, the most prominent highlights are then picked out with pure white.

Many white horses and other darker animals have dapples in the coat colour. In fact dapples are present in almost every colour to some degree, but are much less noticeable on non-greys. Dapples are small, irregular in pattern and generally appear on the rear flanks, sides, lower neck, upper legs and belly; they can also appear over most of the body in some instances. Some patterns are very distinct and others more subtle, fading almost into oblivion. Dapples can range from pure white on a light grey, to a deeper highlight colour on darker horses. Painting them is not as difficult as it may first appear.

Mix the appropriate dapple colour and wait until it is somewhat dry on your palette. Pick up a *very* small amount on the very tip of your brush, and apply just a speck of paint. Carefully feather it outward until it is approximately 1/16in in diameter. Repeat the process in irregular patterns, varying the distinction according to the underlying colour and location of the dapples on the horse. Avoid dappling that is oversized or too regular in pattern; once again, understatement is nearly always better than overkill.

You can enhance Historex horses further with added touches. For example, a horse's muzzle colouring is distinct, ranging from pinkish grey to black depending upon the breed - as always, consult your photo books. Paint the teeth a yellowish white and highlight the lips carefully. The iris of the eye should be dark brown with a black pupil and very little (if any) white showing, unless the horse is frightened or excited. When totally dry, add clear gloss to the entire eye to make it come alive. Also decide if you want to add white facial markings termed tufts, blazes, stars or crescents, depending upon their shape.

I also add a thin shading wash to the tail,

(Below& below right) Claudio Signanini's "Hussar Officer, Royal Guard of Naples"; and snowbound "ADC to Marshal Oudinot", combining Historex and Metal Models parts, which won a Gold Medal at Sévres, 1995.

(Opposite) The author's "Napoleon and Davout", stock kits with extensively reworked anatomy and positioning. Davout was the only Marshal to wear eyeglasses in the field; for this vignette they were made from fine wire with epoxy cement lenses. Note also the detailed embroidery on the waist sash. The Emperor's map was a very small section of a detailed, full-size army map; the collar of his famous greatcoat was extensively reworked for a natural fit.

CHAPTER FOUR: PAINTING

CHAPTER FOUR: PAINTING

(Above left) Claudio Sanchioli's spirited "Neapolitan Dragoon and French Infantryman, 1796"

(Above) "Return from a Charge: 2nd Hussars Officer, 1804" by Claudio Signanini, a Silver Medal winner at Hyères, 1994; note the unusual effect achieved on the hussar's long sidelocks. (Photo Dominique Breffort)

(Left) "Lancer Officer, Kingdom of Naples, 1815" by Ivo Preda, originally the subject of an article in *Figurines* magazine; the rider is almost entirely scratchbuilt and features one of the new Nemrod resin heads. This piece won a Bronze Medal at Sèvres, 1994. (Photo Dominique Breffort)

mane and forelock and let it dry. Drybrush a lighter shade for highlights, and paint in additional highlights on exposed strands. The fetlocks above the hooves also deserve attention: shade the recesses and highlight the fetlocks themselves. Colours in this area can range from the base shade to white if "stockings" are present (also notice that few horses have four perfectly matched white stockings). The hooves themselves also follow a colour pattern, although not so well defined. As you'll see from photos, they range from very dark to very light tans and greys. Historex supply horseshoes; don't paint them bright silver, but use a dark metallic colour or subdued pewter. Paint the underside of the shoe and highlight the horseshoe nails.

Saddlery and harness

The bridle, harness, girth, crupper, breast bands and reins can be various colours. The leather needs to be distinct from the horse's colour. Sometimes this is easy, since senior officers' tack could be of red, gold, white or various other coloured leathers. For troopers, however, the colour was usually brown, black or white. Highlight the areas where the straps curve outwards, and along the top edges. A darker colour can also be added thinly next to the straps to define them better where they lie flat against the horse. Buckles can be dull or bright silver or blackened metal, depending upon the subject. Take special care when painting these since they show up prominently on the completed figure. Add a final touch of clear semi-gloss to all leather.

The saddle is usually painted separately and with as much care as the horse and figure. It is one of those areas that many painters tend to rush but is an important part of any mounted figure. The same basic painting rules apply. First, be absolutely certain that the saddle-to-horse and rider-to-saddle fits are tight and clean. Repairing poor fits after painting has begun is not how you want to spend an evening.

Silver and gold lace is often seen on Napoleonic shabraques and saddlecloths, officers' saddles often being especially ornate with multiple rows of lace trim. Painting lace can be tedious but there are some shortcuts. This is another stage where paint consistency and a well-braced hand pay dividends. For the best results, scrape and sand off the raised lines which Historex includes on these parts; these artificially raised lines only hinder painting, and free-handing is easier for most painters.

If the trim is metallic lace, mix metallic powders or inks with small amounts of oils to get a creamy consistency that flows easily from the brush (white or grey with silver powder, and yellow or yellow ochre with gold powder). I prefer using this matt metallic mixture to paint the entire area first, adding the dividing lines between rows of lace when dry. An added advantage is that mistakes in painting the dividing lines are easily corrected since the powder/oil paint mixture is very opaque.

Valises, rolled saddle blankets, baggage or extraneous gear should be painted separately and attached later when dry so they will not interfere when painting other areas. I prefer drilling a hole in the under-surfaces for temporary attachment to a toothpick, thus giving me a temporary painting handle which can easily be removed later.

When the saddle assembly is painted, look for additional areas to bring out the details, including ornamentation, the saddle's edges and ridges, and larger flat surfaces which can be enhanced by shading and highlighting. Remember that the miscellaneous leather

"General Colbert" by Shep Paine. (Photo Lane Stewart)

CHAPTER FOUR: PAINTING

Beautifully painted detail in Claudio Signanini's "Evening of Friedland". (Photo Dominique Breffort)

straps need a coat of semi-gloss varnish. The finished product should then receive the same weathering treatment as the figure, dry-brushing the basic groundwork colour up the lower extremeties with oils or pastels. Again, err on the side of restraint; but check your references for a photo of a horse which has been galloping over soft going, and you will see just how high hooves can kick up gouts of mud. Remember that Napoleonic cavalry forded rivers as often as using bridges; and that a column of several hundred horse trotting along a dirt road in high summer sends up clouds of powdery dust just like a truck convoy.

*   *   *

There are a few other items which deserve special mention when painting. Probably the most daunting are the **pelisses and dolmans** worn by Napoleonic light cavalry, which are replete with rows of lace and buttons. When your cavalryman is following the fashion of wearing his pelisse slung over one shoulder and a dolman beneath, you face the same painting challenge twice on one figure. There is no short cut - in smaller modelling scales these items represent extended painting time. Historex's representation of these parts is very precise and complete, meaning there is a lot to paint. The first word of advice is, obviously, to study the pelisse and/or dolman carefully, using higher magnification to paint them if your eyes fail you.

Undercoat these parts with acrylics (I use Polly-S) in the basic colour, starting with a *very* thin application to avoid obscuring the fine moulded detail. Next, using the thinned mixture of a darker shading colour, carefully outline all raised lace, letting the paint run into the crevices and recesses of the lace. Outline the entire area around the buttons, inside the rows of lace, and other raised detail. Now paint the rest of the garment, leaving the major lace detail until the last (I don't like to risk a careless brush over completed lace).

The lace itself is painted with the appropriate colour, thinning the paint consistency as much as possible. The only method I've found effective is to carefully paint each row, keeping the lines as straight as your hand allows. You can always come back and make corrections, but try to get it right the first time to avoid paint build-up. Finally, go back over the rows of

CHAPTER FOUR: PAINTING

(Above left) "General Krasinski, 1812" by Ivo Preda combined a Historex horse with Le Cimier's foot figure reworked into a rider, with a scratchbuilt saddle and harnessing.

(Above) "Foot Artillery of the Guard and Engineer of the Guard" by Shep Paine.

"Trumpet Major, 2nd (Dutch) Lancers of the Guard" by Dr Mike Thomas, a long-time exponent of Historex whose award-winning work has often appeared in modelling publications over the years.

CHAPTER FOUR: PAINTING

CHAPTER FOUR: PAINTING

(Above) General view and enlarged detail from a meticulously painted Historex figure of "General Colbert" by Adrian Bay, currently one of the United Kingdom's top painters.
(Photos Phil Kessling)

(Left) Another well-known British modeller and Historex pioneer is Max Longhurst; that his "Officer, 5th Hussars" will stand this sort of enlargement is a tribute to his precise painting style.

(Left inset) Greg DiFranco's "Colonel Lepic at Eylau", inspired by the magnificent Detaille painting of the Horse Grenadiers of the Guard.
(Photo Bill Horan)

buttons with a slightly darker shade, painting a thin "line" down the rows of buttons. Let this dry and then come back to dot in the buttons themselves. It takes practice and patience, but few figures match a hussar in full splendour.

Painting stripes down trouser legs or onto jackets is easier if, again, you remove at the clean-up stage any raised lines moulded onto the figure. Try to ensure that the initial striping colour is very opaque to avoid paint build-up. If the trousers are lighter than the stripe, use a complimentary colour to outline the sides of the stripes. Complex knots, loops or chevrons of lace can also be painted onto the figure, which produces a better result than the parts supplied for this ornamentation. For Hungarian knots of lace or other intricate patterns, I pencil the outline onto the figure first; this allows me to get the shape and location of the lace correctly positioned without the somewhat awkward task of gluing these very delicate parts into place. I discard these parts simply because I find it easier and more realistic to paint the designs.

Too often we see **weapons** painted less carefully than the rest of the figure, spoiling the overall effect. Take the same care to shade, highlight and outline weapons as you would with any other part of the model, carefully picking out the small details. Printer's ink is

CHAPTER FOUR: PAINTING

superior for producing metallic tones, and it can be mixed with oil paints. The pigment in printer's ink is extremely fine, exhibits almost no graininess and flows freely. Remember that a very small amount goes a long way, especially when mixed with clear gold size as the medium.

Using this same procedure, it is relatively easy to produce various textures of metallic lace. Even officers' bullion lace was not uniformly bright like today's synthetic equivalents; it tarnished in recesses, and should be shaded and highlighted like any other part of the figure. A wash of the complimentary shading can be applied into recesses no matter how small; when dry, highlights can be picked out with lighter shades, or pure metallic colour on officers' lace made from (or some NCOs' lace interwoven with) bullion wire threads.

(Above left) Note the mud colour carefully mixed into the blue of this cloak to "weather" its lower folds. While fresh mud does sometimes cling or cake to the surface of clothing, it is generally more realistic to modify the actual uniform colour before painting to give an impression of worked-in dirt; for summer dust effects it is essential.

(Above) The masses of lace, cording and buttons on the dolman, pelisse and barrel sash of traditional hussar uniform are one of the most time-consuming challenges for the painter working in small scale. There is no shortcut; for the desired final effect nothing works except unremitting patience - every strand must be of consistent size and consistently shaded and highlighted.

CHAPTER FOUR: PAINTING

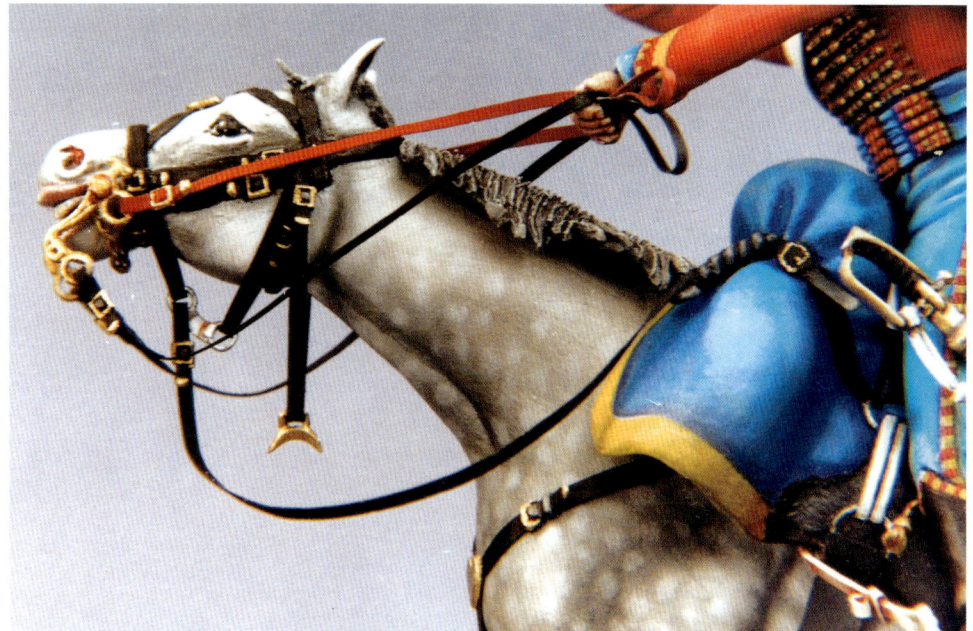

(Left) Dapples have been applied to the horse's neck and shoulder as small, irregular patches which are feathered into the darker grey of the coat.

(Left) Each button on the pelisse is separately painted. Note also that the sleeves have been hollowed out, and all fur roughened with the pyrogravure and highlighted during the painting.

(Bottom left) Saddlery - like this Carabinier's officer's horse furniture - must be shaded and highlighted as carefully as the figure and the horse. Like clothing and horseflesh, a furnished saddle is a complex mass made up of various curved and compound surfaces, displaying variously textured materials, and like them its appearance will depend upon the simulation of a consistent light source.

CHAPTER FOUR: PAINTING

(Left) Long runs of striping on e.g. trousers and horse furniture must be of consistent width; any variation shows up badly, since the stripes are normally in bright colours against a shadowed or outlined background. It is actually easier to achieve this if you remove any raised striping moulded into the plastic parts during the clean-up phase.

(Right) "Officer, Lancers of Berg" by the author. Note the horse's sheen as compared to the flatter colours of the rider's uniform. The silver lace stripes down the trousers were painted with a mixture of silver powder and white oil paint, which has excellent covering power. The shabraque has also been shaded and highlighted, including the folds in the silver lace edging.

CHAPTER FIVE
GROUNDWORK & DISPLAY

Displaying the result of many hours of work to its best advantage means locating the right base, and creating a realistic setting for your figure. When selecting a permanent base pick the best you can afford; there are many relatively inexpensive lines of good-looking wooden bases available, and the appeal of Napoleonic figures is always enhanced by a quality base.

The only rule to bear in mind when selecting a size is to be careful not to "over-base" the model, whether single foot, single mounted, or a group. Too large a base overshadows the immediate visual impact of the model itelf; and it can adversely affect the composition. If anything, I try to slightly "under-base" my miniatures, not only to dramatize the figure itself, but also to limit the groundwork to just enough to make the scene interesting. Vignettes and dioramas look best if the setting is an adjunct to the figures, and not so large or "busy" as to distract the viewer's eye from that central focus. Every item on the base should direct the viewer's attention to the main subject. Random inclusion of equipment, debris and foliage can clutter the setting without adding interest.

Start by looking carefully at the base you've selected. Given the inevitable slight differences of colour, grain or finish and mild wear-and-tear each base will usually have a "best side", which should face the viewer when the figure is attached. (Remember, again, that you begin the painting process by attaching the figure to a temporary base. Don't mount the figure on the permanent base for painting, or by the time you've finished the amount of paint smeared onto the base will ruin its appearance.)

Also remember that all groundwork, debris or miscellaneous items should be in scale to Historex. It can be very tempting to include scenic material or accessories even if they are too large or too small; if they are out of scale, however, they will detract rather than add to

A well-known conversion by Shep Paine of "Dutch Lancers of the Guard", the dramatic effect increased by raising the scene onto a bank overhanging a small gully. (Photo Lane Stewart)

the overall affect. The same applies to the groundwork. For example, thick strands of hemp "grass" or oversized smooth stones look out-of-place simply because they are not in scale with the figure or with nature.

Keep in mind that the setting does not have to be elaborate in every case. Much depends on the figure and the effect you are trying to create. Be certain that the setting does not overwhelm the figure. A lace-encrusted general officer can be effectively placed in a simple, unadorned setting without losing his impact. On the other hand, a rather plain infantryman can be enhanced by standing among village rubble, or in a dry creek bed.

Think about the historical locale as you plan the groundwork for your scene. At the period of the uniform depicted, did the regiment represented by your figure fight on the dusty

CHAPTER FIVE: GROUNDWORK & DISPLAY

CHAPTER FIVE: GROUNDWORK & DISPLAY

(Left inset) Joe Videcki's "Reflections", a Grenadier of the 3rd Swiss Infantry of the Grande Armée, imaginatively posed and displayed. Remember that soldiers did not spend all their time on campaign.

(Left) "LaSalle": Ivo Preda's model of the legendary brigade commander of the French 5th and 7th Hussars provides an excellent example not only of the high standard of painting among today's Italian miniaturists, but also of ambitious groundwork. The dried-out "treetrunk" is the sort of thing that you can find in any garden or park if you train your eye to "see in scale". Note the convincingly rusty chain draped around the shattered gun wheel, with its separating iron tyre.

(Above left) This Sapper of Grenadiers, painted by Larry Munné, leans casually on a Historex frontier marker accessory.

(Above right) "The Sharp End" by the author, a moment of combat between a French Line Lancer and a Russian Cuirassier. This is a good illustration of the extremes of movement and tension possible with Historex conversions; of the added impression of space which may sometimes be obtained by extending the figure out from the edge of a small base; and of the convincing battlefield effect which can be created by careful groundwork over even the most limited area.

summer plains of Spain, or mired in the mud of a wet German autumn? Is he riding, carefree, through springtime France, or retreating through the snow of Poland? If you're depicting a particular individual, battle, or event then it's worth some research to identify the appearance of the specific terrain, the season and the weather conditions.

Terrain application

Not every figure needs to be placed on a flat base or level terrain. If the setting is outdoors the ground will usually be irregular, and creating the underlying terrain offers opportunities to practice your landscaping talents. For example, by slightly exaggerating the ground elevation above the base a more dramatic effect can be achieved. With a little imagination you can create a small raised cliff or, taking the opposite approach, a sunken gully. With careful planning such effects can be achieved even on a small base.

The first step is to create the basic contours of the terrain. This can be done with any number of materials, or the base itself can be carefully

CHAPTER FIVE: GROUNDWORK & DISPLAY

(Right) Groundwork can give scope for imagination and care even on a single-figure base. This detailed stump is a product of Armand P. Bayardi, painted with the same care as the figure. Note the etched brass ferns and the static grass.

(Left) The snow shown here is an initial application of white A+B putty, spread with an additional layer of acrylic modelling paste. The lumps in the snow are partially dry pieces of the paste added while the mixture was still wet.

(Right) Small added touches can be effective, as shown by the destroyed road sign and strewn wood. It is sometimes tempting to add too much: always remember that the spectator's eye should be drawn immediately to the central figure, not distracted by too much fussy peripheral detail.

CHAPTER FIVE: GROUNDWORK & DISPLAY

(Right) The irregular stonework here is actually a small section of a plastic sheet simulating stones, as available in many hobby shops. The section was embedded into the groundwork, with water-soluble white glue added between the individual stones and around the edges. The normal mixture of gutter dirt and static grass was then sprinkled between the stones, simulating the grass and moss growing up among the metalling of a centuries-old European roadway.

(Right) The paving blocks on the base of the author's "Crusader" figure were made from Sculpey, a malleable sculpting material, but the same effect can be achieved with several other modelling mediums.

(Right) The pavement for street scenes can be produced using commercially available stonework embossed on plastic sheets. In this instance the stones have been raised on a balsawood plank and extended down the sides with A+B putty to add depth. Take the time to paint the stones individually, varying the shades, shadowing and highlighting.

CHAPTER FIVE: GROUNDWORK & DISPLAY

Bill Horan, USA:

"I came upon Historex kits and accessories relatively late in my modelling experience. My first figures were World War II plastic figures and the early Airfix Waterloo series, Historex parts being unavailable where I lived at the time. My first exposure to them in the late 1970s was a bit of a revelation. The densely packed plastic packages contained all sorts of fascinating little parts, from heads and legs to microscopic numbers, letters and devices. These seemed to offer the miniaturist a wealth of potential figure, vignette and diorama ideas, as well as the ability to depict even the most minute detail in 54mm.

"My own historical interests lay primarily in other areas, particularly the British Colonial period and the American Civil War, so I rarely diversified into Historex kit building or their conversion in the fashion made famous by Ray Lamb, Shepard Paine and many others. Yet there is no doubt that without the superb Historex work of these artists to shoot for, I might never have had the confidence to delve into the conversion of plastic figures, and ultimately the creation of my own original pieces. Even now the occasional Historex part finds its way into my figures. More than anything else, it was the exciting possibilities that Historex offered the miniaturist that I believe will stand as their legacy within the hobby."

Bill Horan's French Dragoon leads his horse along a wet, muddy track; note the realistic scale appearance of the fallen branches.

chiselled or cut into an irregular surface. Since a single Historex figure is relatively small, I prefer using A+B putty to provide the initial contours. Celluclay (a form of papier-maché) is economical for larger areas. It mixes easily if a few drops of liquid soap and Elmer's Glue are added, which also aid adhesion. If a thick application is made of any material you should check for shrinkage, cracks or distortion after it dries. These are easily corrected by the addition of more material before painting begins, but allow two or three days for the initial application to dry. Carefully and neatly "feather" the terrain to the base's outer edges, being especially careful not to mar the base. I keep a cup of clean water on my worktable just to clean my hands when adding groundwork or handling the base.

Surface materials

The opportunities for creative use of various materials to produce realistic groundwork are limited only by the modeller's imagination. I have seen just about everything used effectively, including kitty-litter, roots, shale, floral decorations, and coal. Keep your eyes open for odd bits and pieces that can be incorporated into groundwork; I look for suitable material when I'm playing golf or taking walks, often ending up with pockets full of twigs and stones.

Since most settings are fairly simple or generic in nature, the best ground cover is what is termed "gutter dirt". If you look closely as you walk along a street you'll often see fine sand and debris next to the kerb; scoop up some in a box or jar, later removing bits of glass, oversize pebbles and unusable trash. This leaves a mixture of sand, fine dirt, small pebbles, twigs and bits of wood, most of which are in perfect scale. Separate the larger pebbles and twigs into another container and save them. What's left is the best ground cover you can use - and it's free.

The process of adding this material to the terrain begins with an undiluted layer of white glue brushed evenly onto the base. White glue tends to run where you don't want it, so take your time and work from the centre outward, covering about one square inch at a time. Generously sprinkle the dirt onto the wet glue and tamp it down gently with a dampened finger. Place something like a shoe box underneath the base to catch the excess gutter dirt as you apply it; tilt the base and gently tap it to remove the loose dirt. Repeat this process, covering small areas during each application until the base is covered.

CHAPTER FIVE: GROUNDWORK & DISPLAY

(Above left) Even smaller scenes can be "elevated" to add a touch of drama. The effect of a small gully is simply achieved here by undercutting the groundwork.

(Above) Scattered gutter dirt, small stones, tiny twigs and, in this instance, a shattered shako and a suitably aged bayonet are painted and drybrushed with acrylics.

You can place rocks and twigs into position while the glue is wet; larger holes for fence posts, road signs, etc. can be drilled once the glue/dirt mixture has dried. Select all terrain and foliage features with care, and - as always - get your eye in by studying photos or paintings if you don't have actual experience of the correct type of terrain. It is horribly easy to destroy the scale effect by, say, putting rounded, water-smoothed pebbles in a grassland setting where big round rocks would never occur in nature. Inspect the groundwork carefully once you've finished, and patch up any bare spots that might remain with additional glue and dirt.

To replicate grass and weed groundcover the most realistic material is static grass. This comprises countless minute threads of fibre material, usually sold in plastic packets in a bilious (and totally unsuitable) green colour which has to be overpainted after application. It is very uniform in length, but can be enhanced by a material which is sold under the name of "Field Grass" produced by Woodland Scenics; cut and mix longer strands of this material with the static grass for variation. (These materials can be found in hobby shops, model railroad shops, and most mail-order modelling houses.)

As with gutter dirt, applying static grass is not a neat process; I use the shoe box to catch the overflow and keep it from invading the crevices of my worktable. These tiny fibres have a nasty habit of appearing later on wet paint. If you decide to add your figure to the base before completing the groundwork, be certain that the painted model is completely dry before applying static grass.

The best results are obtained by first adding the gutter dirt and painting it a dark brownish-green before applying static grass. Next, brush white glue onto the area where you want to add the grass. Take a pinch of it between your fingers and press it into the glue, gently tapping the excess off into the box and blowing

CHAPTER FIVE: GROUNDWORK & DISPLAY

(Left) A Historex conversion by Ivo Preda, "Major, Lithuanian Regiment, 1813", depicting Mustapha Mura Achmatowitz. The attractive groundwork includes one detail too often forgotten - remember that most campaigning took place in spring and summer, when the meadows and roadsides of pre-pesticide Europe were alive with wild flowers.

the remaining loose strands away. Repeat the process several times, and let the glue dry before painting the grass.

Small bits of rotted wood and twigs have a variety of uses. Plant roots such as crabgrass, azalea, or almost any small plant can be dried and used as small leafless shrubs. Most settings do not require massive amounts of plant life, but a few simple twigs or small roots inserted into the groundwork while it's still wet will add variety.

Besides groundwork, there are any number of special touches that add life to your setting. If you include **battlefield debris**, make certain that it does not sit lightly atop grassy areas - remember that such things have weight, are grimy, and may be broken or even partially buried. Favourite items with many modellers - because available in scale - are bits of wrecked cannons, wagons, etc. A wagon or cannon wheel is a brutally heavy piece of timber and iron, whose own weight will press it into soft ground; this is even more true of a cannon barrel, which can weigh up to half a ton. Such items should be painted first and then positioned while the groundwork is still wet, allowing parts to be pressed down into the surface. (Remember, when painting, that although brass barrels merely dull, in damp weather any unpainted or newly exposed iron in the open air starts to rust in 24 hours.)

Napoleonic armies marched on metalled roads where they could, but most European minor roads were unsurfaced; they quickly became churned quagmires in wet weather, and mazes of dust-filled, concrete-hard ruts in the dry, so armies always spread out onto the fields beside the roads. Constructing different types of rail **fences** from balsa or bass wood - or even a single fencepost and broken rail - adds another touch of interest that doesn't take a lot of extra work. Small square and flat strips of wood can be made into posts and rails. Cut them to size, sand them, add a coat of acrylic paint and leave to dry; re-sand the wood, and add another thin coat of paint. You can make the wood appear old or worn, weathering it by shading and highlighting; you'll find that greys and light tans are more realistic than dark browns. (Railroad modelling shops may carry lines of paint which include weathered wood finishes.)

There are several lines of precast **landscape and architectural accessories** available from modelling mail order houses which may be suitable for Napoleonic settings, either straight from the packet or suitably converted; but - once again - be very careful to avoid anachronistic scale relative to Historex models. For further ideas, hit the library and find books which give you a chance to study paintings from life of Napoleonic period European scenes. Pumps and water troughs were always magnets for campaigning soldiers, particularly horsemen. In many parts of Europe simple roadside calvaries were common. It was the cavalry of campaigning armies which were sent out over the fields to forage, and stooks and ricks of various local shapes appear in many period paintings. There is really no end to the possibilities, but always keep in mind the golden rule: the "props" are there to set off your miniature soldier, not the other way round, so don't let such incidentals overwhelm the figure, however pleased you are to have found or sculpted them.

Snow is another effective setting, but one which many modellers find challenging. Every conceivable medium has been tested over the years - flour, baking soda, various putties,

CHAPTER FIVE: GROUNDWORK & DISPLAY

spackle, plaster and marble dust, or alum powder are just a few of the solutions advanced. I have never been a keen advocate of loose, powdery mediums, simply because most lack "staying power", and many have a tendency to discolour over time. My preference is to use either plain white A+B putty, or Acrylic Modelling Paste by Liquitex (available in most art stores).

The application is relatively simple. Either of these mediums can be laid over the entire terrain or in patches, smoothed with a wet brush for an even texture. Hoof and foot prints can be pressed into the surface while still wet. Next, small lumps of partially dried acrylic paste are added to simulate snow which has been disturbed. When totally dry the snow can be shaded with delicate applications of *very* pale blue for a truly cold appearance. As a final touch, a very small sprinkling of minutely ground up glass beads can be added into thin washes of white glue; careful brushing of this mixture over the "snow" provides an icy sparkle. Additional twigs or small shrubs can be inserted, and the whole affair set aside to dry. Careful application of Five Minute epoxy to branches is effective for simulating icicles.

If you prefer more **urban settings**, plastic sheets of cobble-stone and brick surfaces can be purchased to simulate metalled roadway, or you can make them yourself using A+B putty. Care in painting stones or brickwork should equal the effort lavished on the figure or other groundwork. You need to have a critical eye, striving to bring even stonework to life; this means careful painting of individual stones, bricks, crevices and mortar work, with subtle highlighting and shading to add depth and dimension.

If the entire surface is stonework, glue a thin sheet of wood beneath the stonework to raise the surface slightly, and add putty around the edges. The divisions between the stones can then be extended down the sides so that they appear as solid stones. If an overgrown or abandoned setting is sought, position small areas of stones or bricks, adding weeds and moss in the crevices using static grass.

*   *   *

At this point the figure should still be attached to its temporary painting base. In most instances I complete the painting of the groundwork before adding the figure. Besides avoiding accidentally spattering the figure while painting the groundwork, there are practical reasons for completing the groundwork first. For example, if a horse is balanced on a single leg then painting the groundwork first

Andrei Koribanics, USA:

"Polish Lancer Kettledrummer" by Andrei Koribanics, with understated but attractive groundwork of weathered stones and grass.

"I remember being exposed to Historex back in the late 1970s at my first MFCA Show. Shep Paine had his notorious 'Red Lancers' vignette on exhibit and I, like everyone else at that show, was blown away by the incredible amount of detail and flamboyant action of the piece. I simply had to know how this miniature piece of art had been executed! On learning that the figures had been created from Historex kits I immediately purchased as many as my meagre funds would allow, along with one of their wonderful catalogues. I still enjoy poring over the photos in that catalogue today - the first true full-colour 'gallery' of miniature art that I can recall. They have served as a great inspiration to me over the years.

"Like most others, I had cut my teeth on cast white metal figures. This styrene medium was somehow both familiar (from my days modelling subjects such as armour and aircraft) and yet new and quite exotic. I was taken by their petite quality and superb detail, qualities very much lacking in the majority of white metal castings at that time. No mere suggestions of braid and other fine detail; it was all there - in a billion pieces, many of which I found difficult to identify, being a connoisseur of neither the French army nor the French language! An additional plus was the little watercolour painting by Eugéne Léliepvre; although perhaps a bit frustrating as a painting guide in and of itself, it was a pretty little addition to a most complete 'package'. Here was everything a modeller needed to execute a faithful rendition of a soldier.

"For me the most exciting advantage of working with Historex kits is the fact that they are easily cut, filed and sanded, and therefore easily modified. I enjoy making one-of-a-kind pieces, focusing particularly on highly animated action, and here styrene is a most accommodating medium, much more so than white metal. With a wide assortment of body parts (both human and horse), an unlimited range of possibilities is available to the modeller for both subject matter and animation. Of course, the detail parts always have been exquisite. The finely moulded swords, trumpets, buckles, etc. lend themselves to endless conversion possibilities. Although it has been a while since I've built a Historex kit straight from the bag, I still find myself digging through my spares box for the occasional detailed part to add to a scratchbuilt piece.

"Ironically, I also remember that in the 'old days' there was a perception among figure collectors that the fact that Historex figures were styrene somehow made them intrinsically less substantial and therefore less valuable than their white metal counterparts. It was as if white metal had intrinsic value, much in the way a snobbish art collector will suggest that a work in acrylics is less valuable than a work in oils! It is readily evident by the work seen here, however, that in the hands of a gifted artist the results transcend the medium."

CHAPTER FIVE: GROUNDWORK & DISPLAY

can avoid your accidentally breaking the leg while manoeuvering with a paintbrush.

Paint static grass with a thin wash of acrylic or even oil paint, feathering the colour into the surrounding groundwork. Don't use too much paint or the static grass will become a matted mess. Highlight it with a paler shade of green and then a light yellowish green/tan colour drybrushed onto the extreme tips only.

Painting the remainder of the groundwork is a relatively simple process. I use Polly-S or any other acrylic, but be careful: too much paint or too many washes can loosen the groundwork. Interesting variations can be added if lighter shades of browns are flowed into the base colour while the paint is still wet. The next step is drybrushing the terrain. Start with a medium highlight colour over the darker base colour described earlier. Lightly brush it across the groundwork surface, using just enough pressure to transfer the almost-dry paint onto the upper surfaces only. Repeat the process with a lighter shade, then again with a still lighter mix. Larger rocks and small stones should be painted individually using greys and light tans, remembering to highlight and shade them. When the entire ground cover is painted, let it dry, and inspect it again the next day. There may be small areas that need to be corrected or repaired.

Take a careful look at the finished base and mentally position the figure before permanently attaching it. Remember that better composition is achieved by setting the figure at an angle rather than parallel to the edges of the base. When the position is selected, drill oversized holes into the groundwork to attach the figure.

Take your time attaching the figure and ensure that it is not leaning. The pins protruding from the feet or hooves should fit loosely into the holes, allowing some leeway for final adjustment. Too tight a fit can result in breakage if you try to force the figure into an upright or slightly different position. Use Five Minute epoxy to secure the figure since this will allow you sufficient time to position it correctly. If the holes need to be re-drilled, simply fill the old holes with a pinch of gutter dirt or a small stone and touch up the area.

Always check the fit beneath the feet and hooves one final time. Since the groundwork is comprised of uneven material, you may need to add more filler. To do this, apply white glue in the space with a toothpick and sprinkle a coating of the finer gutter dirt around and beneath the foot or hoof. Use a dampened old brush to clean away excess groundwork from the shoes, and repaint the area when it dries.

"Roger's Ranger, 1776" by Etienne Ducarme, in the ambitious and splendidly achieved setting of a typical north-east American birch swamp. This is an example of a model in which the groundwork is as important to the overall effect as the human figure; it is a risky choice to make, but can be stunning if you have the skill and patience to pull it off. (Photo Dominique Breffort)

The final touch is to add to the figure or horse any miscellaneous and loose items still remaining - the reins, lance, slung carbine, or any item which would have interfered with painting. I prefer to add these delicate pieces during the very last stage of construction to avoid damaging them, and it's easier to handle the figure and mount it into final position if they are out of harm's way. Touch up these items after they are attached or if they require more definition.

The most ambitious groundwork of all – see the photo above – is the mini-diorama in which your figure is deliberately almost overwhelmed by very complex vegetation or other effects; its appeal lies in the air of danger for the isolated figure. This book is no place for detailed instruction on scenic effects; but if you have the references, the materials and the courage, it is an exciting challenge.

CHAPTER SIX
NON-NAPOLEONIC CONVERSIONS

Although it would be impractical to attempt to "talk the reader through" the detailed assembly of the conversions pictured in this chapter, no celebration of Historex would be complete without at least illustrating a representative selection of non-Napoleonic subjects. I believe these will convey to the reader better than any words the astonishing versatility of these products. All of these figures involved Historex to a greater or lesser degree.

The sheer volume of available parts and accoutrements provide an excellent basis for drastic conversions. Once some of the techniques involved in converting figures are mastered the modeller has access to an unlimited number of subjects and periods. While these are drastic departures from the company's original intent, this approach has produced an array of award-winning figures which would otherwise have been virtually unattainable.

Historex's consistent anatomy is an important feature for converters. Some may retain some of the moulded detail on the body parts, but in many instances most of it is removed. This produces an unadorned mannequin, bare of uniform but assuring the experienced modeller of accurate proportions over which a new uniform and other details can then be recreated with putty and a variety of other materials. Others have progressed to scratchbuilding "from the ground up", but retain their affection for the spare parts available - and particularly for the horses. Bill Horan, for instance, might use only a helmet, horse or weapon, preferring to create his own body parts. On the other hand, Ivo Preda of Italy often uses most of the Historex kit; or may combine a heavily modified metal figure with a Historex horse for an entirely new mounted figure. Other modellers, like Joe Berton, have created totally new subjects, using Historex to varying degrees as the basis for both military and civilian figures.

Conversions from Napoleonic to mid-19th century subjects are sometimes fairly straightforward. This is an "Officer, 2nd Dragoons, Balaclava 1856" by Martin Livingstone.

CHAPTER SIX : NON-NAPOLEONIC CONVERSIONS

(Left) Joe Videcki's "Mountain Men" could hardly be further from the precise formality of Napoleonic uniform; they are, nevertheless, Historex conversions.

(Below) An excellent example of the conversion possibilities to non-Napoleonic subjects is this medieval boxed diorama, "At the Well" by Glyn Porteous.

CHAPTER SIX : NON-NAPOLEONIC CONVERSIONS

(Left) "Robert E. Lee", a scratchbuilt figure by Bill Horan, includes a converted Historex horse as Traveller. (Photo Bill Horan)

(Below) Horan's fine scratchbuilt "Major General John A. Logan" (Photo Bill Horan)

CHAPTER SIX : NON-NAPOLEONIC CONVERSIONS

(Above left) Beautifully converted "Moghul Cavalryman" by Martin Livingstone, as seen at the 1996 Chicago Show.

(Above right) Martin Livingstone's "Turenne, Marshal of France", on a rarely seen piebald horse.

(Left) "Lord Bingham, Colonel 17th Lancers, 1825" by Bill Horan is a prime example not only of his conversion, scratchbuilding and painting skills, but also of the adaptability of Historex. (Photo Bill Horan)

(Opposite above) Revolutionary War conversion by Dr Preston Russell: "The Philadelphia Light Horse".

(Opposite below) Russell's "Les Misérables", a rare example of a vignette inspired by a theatrical set.

CHAPTER SIX : NON-NAPOLEONIC CONVERSIONS

Philadelphia Light Horse 1776

Dr Preston Russell, USA:

"After years of tormenting Historex parts for conversions I have come to think of them as old friends, even if a bit carved-up, mutilated and burned beyond recognition. There they sit in multiple little drawers, obedient for the moment, awaiting transformation into the next battle: heads in this drawer, arms in that, muskets here, helmets there - thousands of little white fragments awaiting their call to duty. . .

"How I love the horse parts, their right halves crammed into one drawer and their left into another, heads in a third, already prancing, galloping or sprawling in my mind. Seized by some new vision of thundering hooves (the Crimea? Lauzun's Legion at Yorktown? Pulaski's Last Charge?), I splay out little virginal white bodies all over the table. What - no flailing rear legs left in the drawer? Back to the catalogue, mixing and matching, plotting to saw No.16 in half to match the rear quadrant with a startled No.9.

"I recall some long-suffering Historex dealer like Bob Santos, picking through his mountainous bins of inventory to fill up one little plastic bag with six No.319s, twelve No.502s, seven No.275s, and oh yes - send me some of those great carbines, plus some more horseshoes. . . The different combinations range into the hundreds to produce 'just that horse' for the occasion - some paper clip joints here, a little epoxy putty there, and voila!

"The horse, clearly a thoroughbred, has a placid expression, particularly for one which might just have had a cannonball whizz past it; but putting the ears on backwards is a great start to reversing its grazing complacency. A little putty work on the eyes and nostrils summons up a scared-stiff look. And if you can still find them, you can always substitute the heads from other manufacturers like Airfix. Given such a great start by the basic Historex parts, one does not have to be a Grand Master to design ones own horse - just that one, perfect horse for that particular moment in history.

"As the hours pass you may even find yourself talking to it as the little life form evolves under your fingers. But if it starts talking back, it might be time to consider an afternoon of golf; like a faithful pet, it will still be there when you return."

A collector of old English horse paintings, Dr Preston Russell reproduced a Stubbs in three dimensions in his delightful "The Prince of Wales's Saddle Horses".

CHAPTER SIX : NON-NAPOLEONIC CONVERSIONS

(Right) "Flash'd While They Turn'd in Air..." by Greg DiFranco was a Best of Show winner at Chicago, evoking the Tennyson poem on the Charge of the Light Brigade at Balaclava. (Photo Lane Stewart)

(Left) In a completely different mood, DiFranco's delicate "Garibaldi's Mandolinist" was another show winner. It seems deceptively simple, until you take time to study the impeccable conversion work and painting. (Photo Lane Stewart)

(Right) Dr Preston Russell's "Charge of the Light Brigade" captures the moment of a fatefully misunderstood conversation.

CHAPTER SIX : NON-NAPOLEONIC CONVERSIONS

(Right) "Roman Rider" by Shep Paine - a scene straight out of a John Ford movie, and a famous demonstration of Shep's pioneering animation work and "stage management". The near horse appears to be totally suspended in mid-air; it is supported, via the rider's feet, by the far horse's single grounded hoof. With pinned connections to strengthen the joins, Historex's lightweight material allows almost any degree of airborne animation which the modeller can think up.

(Left) Martin Livingstone's 12th century "Templar at Bay" has a most convincing sense of movement; note also the skilfully handled ringmail hauberk and the lightweight appearance of the thin surcoat.

(Right) A superb rendition of the "Consecration of John of Gaunt" by Ray Anderson, one of the classic Historex conversions.

CHAPTER SIX : NON-NAPOLEONIC CONVERSIONS

(Above left) Joe Berton's delightful "Ascent of the Great Pyramid", one of the author's all-time favourite Historex conversions, not only for its gentle comedy but for the skilfully achieved interaction of the different figures.

(Above) Joe Berton's "War in the Sudan, 1884" pursues his great interest in the Middle East, with an ambitious conversion to one of the astonishingly medieval-looking riders still to be seen on late 19th century battlefields.

(Left) An early conversion by the author, "Crusader", paired a Men-at-Arms figure with a heavily converted Historex horse. Note that the length of the horse's legs has been increased and the fetlocks enlarged.

CHAPTER SIX : NON-NAPOLEONIC CONVERSIONS

(Above) "A Moi! Mousquetaire Gris, Steenkerke, 1693" by Martin Livingstone, a worthy Gold Medal winner at the Paris Mondial in 1996. (Photo Dominique Breffort)

(Above right) " Samurai", a heroically radical conversion superbly painted, won Jacques Ingret a Gold Medal at the Paris Mondial in 1996. (Photo Dominique Breffort)

(Right) Hervé de Belenet's "Saldjukid Falconer", a Gold Medal winner at both Sèvres 1995 and Mondial 1996. (Photo Dominique Breffort)

CHAPTER SIX : NON-NAPOLEONIC CONVERSIONS

(Above left & right) Martin Livingstone's award-winning "Gallic Chieftain, 3rd Century BC" and 11th Century "L' Oriflamme", at the 1996 Chicago Show.

(Left) "Les Chemins de Savenay, 1793", by Jean-Marc Couetoux, sets these counter-revolutionary scouts perfectly in relation to the groundwork and each other to tell a visual "story".

(Opposite top) The sacred, and the profane..."Joan of Arc", and "Monsieur est servi", both by Christian Legros.

(Opposite bottom) Philippe Gengembre's converted Historex figures of 16th century Anglo-Scottish "Border Reivers" earned him Gold at the Paris Mondial, 1996.
(All photos Dominique Breffort)

(OVERLEAF) A superb action piece, "Montgomery Falls 1759" by Etienne Ducarme won a Gold at AMC 1995 and was featured on the cover of *Figurines* magazine. Its courageous conception and impeccable conversion, animation, painting and groundwork make it a fitting candidate to close this brief review of the extraordinary versatility of Historex. (Photo Dominique Breffort)

CHAPTER SIX : NON-NAPOLEONIC CONVERSIONS

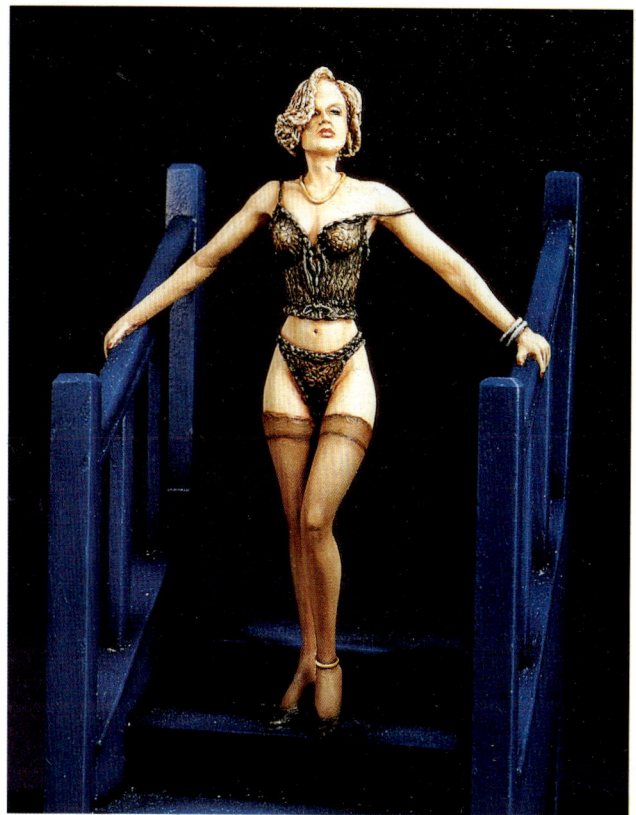

NOTE ON SUPPLIERS
The following are just a few of the major suppliers' addresses which may be useful to modellers :

USA
The Black Watch, P.O. Box 666, Van Nuys, California 91408, tel (818) 701-5177 (*Historex - mail order only*)
The Red Lancers, 14 Broadway, Milton, Pennsylvania 17847, tel (717) 742-8118 (*Nemrod and newer Historex parts*)
Legends Toys and Hobbies, 1330 Fullerton Road, City of Industry, California 91748, tel (818) 810-8962 (*Historex kits and parts*)
Sentinel Miniatures, 4 Broadway, RM102, Valhalla, New York 10595, tel (914) 682-3932 (*Historex*)
Santos Miniatures, PO Box 4062, Harrisburg, Pennsylvania 17111, tel (717) 545-2949 (*Historex, including parts*)
Stuempfle's Military Miniatures, 13190 Scott Road, Waynesboro, Pennsylvania 17268 (*Historex, old and new*)
Armand P.Bayardi, 544 Pineline Road, Newton, Pennsylvania 18940, tel (215) 598-8102 (*groundwork and architectural elements*)
Thomas Art Bases, Ken Thomas, 1909 Woodstream Drive, York, Pennsylvania 17402, tel (717) 757-2702 (*bases*)

Great Britain
Historex Agents, Wellington House, 157 Snargate Street, Dover, Kent CT17 9BZ, tel 01314-206720 (*Historex, old and new; Pyrogravure*)
Optum Hobby Aids, PO Box 262, Haywards Heath, W.Sussex RH16 3FR, tel 01444-415027, fax 01444-458606 (*Kneadatite/Duro and Sylmasta/A+B epoxy putties, groundwork supplies, etc.*)
Shesto Ltd., Unit 2 Sapcote Trading Estate, 374 High Road, Willesden, London NW10 2DH (*UMV Swiss micro files, drill tools & accessories, etc.*)

France
NCO Historex, 16, rue Dunoise, 41240 Verdes, tel (16) 54-80-41-76 (*Historex kits and parts, old and new*)
Le 11e Hussard, 15 rue Trousseau, 75011 Paris, tel (1) 47-00-74-33 (*Historex*)

CHAPTER SIX : NON-NAPOLEONIC CONVERSIONS